D1622599

NOBLE PURPOSE

Igniting Extraordinary Passion for Life and Work

BARRY HEERMANN

Printed in the United States of America. The publisher of this book was Paul Scicchitano. It was set in Baskerville and Minion by Suzanne E. Leonard.

About the book cover: "Abundance, Opening to Fullness" was painted by Sister Doris Klein who is a member of the Congregation of the Sisters of St. Agnes. This piece appears in her book, Journey of the Soul (Sheed and Ward, 2000). You can order the book by calling Sheed and Ward at 800-266-5564 or you can see and order other works of Doris Klein by visiting her Web page, www.dorisklein.com.

QSU Publishing Company
3975 University Drive, Suite 230
Fairfax, Virginia 22030 USA
Tel: 703-359-8460; Fax: 703-359-8462
www.qsuonline.com.

Acknowledgements

Far and away the best prize that life offers is the chance to work hard at work worth doing.

— *Theodore Roosevelt*

Colleague Alex Chong frequently refers to Noble Purpose. Critical decisions he makes and his fellow coworkers make is considered in light of this test — "Am I, are we, acting with nobleness of purpose?" I dedicate this book to him, to my wife Kipra, who worked tirelessly, every step of the way in editing this book, and to my editor, Paul Scicchitano, who added wonderful verve and life to this book.

I also wish to acknowledge colleagues who are a part of the Team Spirit community that I am blessed to work with. Team Spirit is a team development program that I created. I dedicate this book to Team Spirit Consultant/Facilitators, organization clients who use Team Spirit and those who show up for Team Spirit Gatherings to celebrate their colleagueship, explore experiences/approaches at the intersection of spirit and team development.

The following people, most of whom are Team Spirit colleagues, generously generated stories about Noble Purpose in their lives, served as reviewers of the Noble Purpose manuscript or supported me along the way in the journey to writing this book: Lora Hein, Nancy Roy, Marsha Snyder, MD, Sharon

Benjamin, Jo Bachman, Gordon Cowperthwaite, Macyl Burke, Peter Jones, Jim Stuart, Cathi Balboa, Jennifer Cash O'Donnell, T. Waldmann-Williams, Judi Neal, Doug Finton, Mike Miller, Lynne Palazzolo, Hank Lindborg, Richard Walsh, Rick Miller, Deborah Vogele Welch, Tim Simmons, Linda Garrett, Kathryn Hall, Steve Hinkle, David Kennebeck, Steve Houchin, Diana Crowell, Cathy Walker, Uwe Weissflog, Mike Arena, Bill Kirkwood, Iris Sauber, Elizabeth Genevieve, Juliana Wisher, Mark Maier, Diane Menendez, Brooke Schneider, Lissa Pohl, Rob St.Germain, Jean Marie Stross, Jennifer Blalock, Jim Balkcom, Mike Travis, Jane Seiling, Belinda Kindschi, Deborah Jacroux and Ellen Burke.

I wish to also acknowledge the first Noble Purpose Study Group participants: Theo and Jude Gladstone Cade, Jan Thompson, David Womeldorf, Dick Genardi and Paula Ray. And I acknowledge old friends serving in leadership positions of major organizations that continue to advise and support me, keeping the flame burning: Stan Sword (Cerner Corporation), Bob Schwiterman (LexisNexis), Rich Glenn (St. Thomas Health Care System), Murray Cohen (The Delphos Hearld and Eagle Print Publishers), Chuck Mallue (Disney Corporation), Rod Goelz (S1), Bruce Bertell (Family Advocacy Services), Mary Miller (Delphi) and Luis Marrero (Disney Corporation).

Finally, I also wish to acknowledge my coaches and mentors, Toni Stone, Bob Ross, Penelope Andrade and David Grudermeyer for their brilliant support.

Blessings to all of you.

Table of Contents

Foreword

My exploration into the extraordinary at work led me to write this book. While the larger culture portrays a pretty grim picture of workplace drudgery, another reality is also true. What is not commonly known is that there are individuals working in teams who report a remarkable sense of passion, beyond anything they had known, coupled with the presence of a powerful quality of spirit and energy in their midst. Individuals in these teams generate exponentially higher levels of performance and service.

The presence of such joy and fulfillment at work is documented in research, including Peter Vaill's investigations into "high performing systems" (*Managing as a Performing Art* 160-171 and 213-222) and the Gallup studies of high performing teams (*First Break All the Rules* 25-34). My work in this domain arises from this research and practice. It is called Team Spirit, and it fosters spirited, high-performing teams (*Building Team Spirit* 17-25). Through this research, and the use of Team Spirit by hundreds of organizational consultants internationally, I have come to appreciate that this knowledge is as critical to individuals as it is to organizations.

In the development of Team Spirit, I immersed myself in the study and practice of spirit that is at the crux of extraordinary teams and individuals. Spirituality is defined in many ways, but often as the search for meaning and purpose in life.

When you come into relationships with meaning in your life, at the deepest level, you are moved, changed and altered. Something emerges in you, or through you, that is life defining. It could be said that you have found meaning. To be infused with meaning calls forth purpose. While meaning has you come alive; purpose requires direction of your energy to the realization of some contribution to others.

Extraordinary workplaces are enlivened by meaning and purpose. Without meaning, it is very difficult to summon forth purpose, and without purpose, what is dear lives only as an inner murmur.

The revealing and discovery of Noble Purpose is assisted through contemplation and reflection. To create the fertile ground for doing this work consider the following:

- Take the time and locate the space, at work, home or in nature for your renewal.
- Allow the silence and the retreat away from habitual routines in your external life and, critically, from the random noise and thoughts of your internal life.
- Quiet your mind.
- Listen for the deeper messages of meaning and purpose.

Noble Purpose will aid your reflection and contemplation. All that is left is that you create the space and time, away from the hustle and bustle of your life, so as to fully enter into the journey to Noble Purpose.

Your satisfaction, pleasure and fulfillment at work is far more in YOUR hands than you might realize. Granted, your workplace may not exhibit, nor may its leaders understand, how to unleash the gifts of Noble Purpose or the passion that exists at the heart of all good work. But, you can. You will return to your essential self, unleashing the distinct meaning and purpose that is original to you. The principles are tried and true, based on solid research and the wisdom of the ages. The rest is up to you.

Part I

CHAPTER 1

Take This Job and Love It

*Keep in mind that a path is only a path; if you feel you should not fol-
low it, you must not stay with it under any condition. This is not an
affront, to oneself or to others, in dropping it if that is what your heart
tells you to do. But your decision to keep on the path or to leave it must
be free of fear or ambition. Try as many times as you think necessary.
Then ask yourself alone, one question. Does this path have heart? ...
One [path] makes for a joyful journey; as long as you follow it, you are
one with it. The other will make you curse life. One makes you strong;
the other weak.*

— *Carlos Castaneda*

A middle-aged "*a ju shi*," as shoeshine operators are commonly called in
Korea, was stooped over a pair of black, worn loafers for what seemed like an
unusually long stretch. The man's much younger customer grew more and
more captivated by what could only be described as a remarkable attention to
detail. Never in the customer's experience had anyone put so much effort into a
simple shoeshine.

Turning to the *a ju shi*, the client asked curiously what motivated this man
to painstakingly visit each seam and crevice on what must have been a sea of

shoes that ebbed by his stained bench each day. Barely adjusting his gaze from the loafers, the man offered this explanation: "Every time I shine a pair of shoes, my kid gets to go to college."

Whether or not he recognized it as such, the man had extraordinary Noble Purpose — something today's most successful corporations prize as the quintessential building stone for establishing a strong sense of corporate social responsibility. This simple man, who probably never traveled more than 50 miles from his birthplace, knew that his legacy would be measured not by the sum of all the loafers he shined in a lifetime but by the opportunity his daily toil brought to his family.

Each time the man dipped his rag into a bucket of shoe wax, his son was closer to becoming a professional — perhaps even a doctor who might one day return sick children to good health. By virtue of his selflessness, the man was rewarded with absolute passion for what some small-minded individuals might see as an undignified living.

What motivates you to show up for work? Is there more waiting for you at the end of a 40-hour workweek than a paycheck? Are you capable of a potentially big contribution that you can't seem to get off the ground? Do you embrace your work life with the *a ju shi*'s passion, or are you merely laying low until retirement?

As children, we often dream about growing up to become astronauts, professional athletes or famous actors, yet very few of us ever reach such lofty heights. Somewhere along our professional and personal life's journey, we accept a much more pragmatic existence, often based on the opportunities at hand. What we do with these opportunities speaks to the very core of who we are and our humaneness to others.

Indeed, Noble Purpose lies within each of us regardless of our social standing or chosen career. Our smallest deeds and words may make a difference not only to our family, friends and coworkers, but quite possibly the entire world.

If you have not yet discovered your Noble Purpose or if you are in touch with your Noble Purpose but you have not been able to satisfactorily bring it to the world, then this book will assist you in manifesting the discovery of your purpose and the means to realize your purpose. The wherewithal to bring your Noble Purpose to fruition lives within, waiting to be revealed and released. This book is essentially about you, returning to your essential self, discovering the perfect wisdom you can contribute to others, fulfilling that which is seeking expression within you.

Many of the great men and women who have gone before you were profoundly in touch with their Noble Purpose — scientists like Jonas Salk, poets like Emily Dickinson, authors like Shakespeare, composers, philosophers, statesmen and dedicated shoeshiners. There is only one absolute: True Noble Purpose must offer the potential of great benefit for someone other than yourself. This doesn't mean that you must always act in a selfless way to have Noble Purpose. However, working with a Noble Purpose that benefits someone other than yourself will allow you to be powerfully rooted to society as a whole. Imagine that today is your last. How would you be remembered? Would your purpose be as selfless as the *a ju shi*'s?

A beautiful Peruvian woman gave up a promising career as a New York City fashion model to work with emotionally and physically disabled children. She later went on to help developing economies build greater economic capacity through improved management practices. Looking back, she recalls the all-too-short life of a 15-year-old boy named Flavio, who succumbed to complications related to Cerebral Palsy and Down Syndrome.

Unable to dress or feed himself, each Saturday the boy was helped into a sports coat by his mother to hand deliver a yellow rose to the beautiful social worker. Though she was responsible for multiple centers and visited more than 100 clients at their homes each week, she always made it a point to drop by the center where Flavio waited sweetly with his rose. He passed away on one such Saturday. And at Flavio's funeral, the woman honored him with a yellow rose. She later drew on his memory to teach understanding and compassion to other social workers.

The former model never looks back on the life she missed by abandoning the runway, nor does she dwell on the personal sacrifice she made to follow her Noble Purpose. On the contrary, she considers how empty her life might have been had she not met Flavio and those she helped through his memory.

While the beautiful social worker changed careers to pursue her Noble Purpose, an American Airlines employee, with an amazing spirit of giving and trust, found a way to fulfill his potential with amazing service to customers.

A 22-year-old Pakistani man arrived at John F. Kennedy International Airport in New York City in the middle of the night after a 16-hour flight from Karachi, Pakistan. He waited patiently in the baggage claim area for a friend with whom his family had arranged for him to stay until he found a job in the United States. After several hours, the American Airlines employee offered to drive the young man to the friend's house on his way home from work. In the car, the airline employee told the man to be suspicious if the friend started making excuses for not picking him up as planned.

When they arrived at the address, the friend looked surprised to see the young man. It soon became apparent that he didn't really want the young man staying with him. The airline employee once again came to the rescue, inviting the young man to room at his place for a few days. His only request was that the man write a short note in his own language of how he benefitted by the act — a note the American Airlines employee wished to add to the dozens of other scribbled messages of gratitude he had collected from wayward travelers over the years. The Pakistani man happily complied. The young immigrant never forgot this unselfish act as he embarked on a successful career in business.

The shoeshiner at the crowded Seoul market, the former model and the American Airlines employee all had their own signature form of Noble Purpose. So do you. The purpose of this book is to assist you in revealing and claiming your Noble Purpose. However, there is one cautionary note — often the moment you begin scanning and evaluating what is missing from your life, it seemingly becomes much more difficult to find. Be assured that you have everything within you to discover your Noble Purpose.

Nobility of Purpose and Moral Action

While there is ample evidence of "survival of the fittest," "winning at all costs" and "might makes right" behavior in the world, it is not the core human instinct. Human beings have a deep longing to contribute and serve. You seek values and beliefs that are big enough to encompass all of your life and work. If you are like most people, at a deep level you are called to serve.

Within Noble Purpose is inherently right action that serves the world, and you are served in the process. Noble Purpose is socially responsible action of the highest order. Behind many successful products or services, there was an initial, authentic impulse to serve and contribute. This motivation to contribute to the common good is moral action at work.

Unfortunately, the originating entrepreneurial idea that gives life to Noble Purpose may be undermined by more self-serving motivations. Great Noble Purpose that spawns a significant product or service has the potential to create a context for unscrupulous behavior. Financial greed is a common manifestation.

Henry Ford observed, "A business that makes nothing but money is a poor kind of business." This is not to claim that fiscal responsibility to stakeholders and the larger community isn't important. It is. At the same time, Noble Purpose transcends that fiscal responsibility.

Noble Purpose that becomes self-serving ceases to be noble. The obligation of people in positions of power in the fulfillment of Noble Purpose, is to be, above all else, good human beings. It means to continually live in the question of what is in the best interest of others, employees, customers, the larger community and the planet.

In the long run, Noble Purpose will succeed to the extent that the right use of power is embraced, redistributing and making accessible the originating Noble Purpose at every level — with colleagues, stakeholders, customers, funding sources, owners and the surrounding community. In the best of all possible worlds, enlightened Noble Purpose, that is fully responsive to the larger community and planet, can be economically successful.

How To Use This Book

This book is intended specifically for professionals, team members and others who seek to embrace their Noble Purpose at work, whether in a profit-making enterprise or helping profession, whether in a technical setting or educational campus, whether working in the arts or practicing a craft. This is not to say that Noble Purpose is exclusively work-related, for it is not. The focus of this book, however, is work as the vehicle for Noble Purpose.

For most of us, work is a place where we spend a significant amount of our time. Work is the canvas where we give expression to our gifts and talents. Work is far more than the source of our livelihood, it is the vessel through which we fashion our identity and contribute to the world around us. Remember, you are not your work. You are infinitely more, and work is a remarkable gift — a channel for you to reveal and express your talents and skills.

While most often the context for the journey to Noble Purpose is work, your professional self is not separate from your personal self. Organizational change is rarely possible without significant personal change of the organization's leaders. Similarly, revealing or empowering Noble Purpose at work is fundamentally about your willingness to change and grow personally. Accordingly, you will be invited to look deeply at formative childhood experiences and beyond, so as to reflect upon your patterned ways of being, perhaps designing new ways for yourself in the world. Thus, this exploration of Noble Purpose at work first requires reformulating the way you have been at a personal level.

This book is organized into two parts. Part I reveals the deep personal roots of Noble Purpose. It discusses how your Noble Purpose can become obscured and what you can do to return yourself to it. Specifically, Chapter Two will explore the Bounded Self, the self that is formed by deep, sometimes more challenging, inner patterns that promote your pursuit of safety, refuge and protection from perceived threats. Accordingly, the Bounded Self may relate to life in a more superficial way.

In Chapter Two, you will also learn about the importance of your Essential Self. The Essential Self is that archetypal, unbounded energy, characterized by an experience of expansive freedom and vitality to create and serve others. It is innately within every one of us.

It is not uncommon to feel out of touch with the expansive freedom and vitality that is the precursor to Noble Purpose. Feeling constrained and diminished is a result of toxicity that obscures or removes you from your Noble

Purpose. And the reverse is true as the absence of Noble Purpose prompts the toxicity. Understanding the Bounded Self Model in Chapter Two and being willing to work with the model will help you return to your Essential Self, to your healing and to service for others.

Part II is designed to help you create the clearing from which your Noble Purpose can take root and flourish. Part II is organized around the six parts of the Noble Purpose Spiral. Each part, or quality, provides the context for revealing and tapping into your Noble Purpose. The tenets of Noble Purpose are intended to be contemplative rather than nice-to-know information or superficial tips.

Each part of the Noble Purpose Spiral, when appropriately combined, leads to remarkable service, personal freedom and fulfillment. The Noble Purpose Spiral offers a process to unlock the door to your gifts and talents. People who have a profound sense of their Noble Purpose regularly and routinely, whether conscious or not, connect with this process. As a result of accessing this process they evolve and expand rather than feel constricted and stymied at work. They have access to their inner strengths by unconsciously transforming the resources available to them into new, creative possibilities. By attending to this process, you are able to brilliantly illuminate and transform the world around you as in the case of our former-model-turned-social-worker.

As the basis of Part II is deep, reflective work, after reading Part I you might want to limit yourself to a single chapter each day thereafter. Start your day with this practice. Then, go back and reflect on the book in its entirety. Allow yourself sufficient time to absorb the deep-rooted implications. Alternatively, you could spend several days on each chapter, reading the text and discussing it with your colleagues. Become part of a Noble Purpose Learning Group, or find a partner with whom you can share your experience. However you decide to pursue Part II of this book, don't treat it as a one-time proposition.

Think of Part II of this book as a practice or a program, not unlike a gymnasium where you would go to develop certain muscles of your body for strength and endurance. The gymnasium offered in this book will develop "muscles" that transform your relationship to work and help you find meaning and purpose.

Each chapter in Part II begins with a short message synthesizing the Noble Purpose quality discussed in that chapter. A schema is highlighted at the end of each chapter to synthesize the major points of discussion. Each chapter concludes with an invitation to create an affirmation — a positive, affirming statement to be repeated throughout the day, to ground the ideas of that chapter. To further integrate the principles expressed in that day's chapter, choose at least one of the following practices:

- An anchoring activity — Invites you to reflect/write about an important theme of that chapter.
- A body exercise — Elicits contemplation of bodily sensations associated with one or more aspects of Noble Purpose.
- A ritual — Offers the opportunity to create a practice to bring to life a particular idea.
- Artistic expression — Suggests the use of art as a way to access your Noble Purpose.
- Journal writing — Proposes journal reflection and writing about some principle in a particular chapter.
- Aesthetic appreciation — Invites you to select between three artistic expressions: music, poetry and painting to rekindle and bring alive the theme of a particular reading.

Some chapters contain an extended process within the chapter, inviting you to reflect more deeply about the particular quality of the Spiral presented. Note that Chapter Eight, on Noble Purpose, contains a particularly lengthy process that requires up to three hours of reflection and journaling.

You will need a pen, paper — ideally a journal or a notebook — and index cards to take into your day with you to record thoughts and affirmations. If you are interested in delving into color, form and more artistic expression, you will want to have colored pens and markers and a drawing journal at hand. We have attempted to build as much consistency as possible among the exercises so that they will become a ready tool in your daily life at home and work.

The purpose of this book, particularly the engagement of the six parts of the Noble Purpose Spiral in Part II, is to keep you enlivened and invigorated over time, creating the space for new and revitalized expressions of your signature form of Noble Purpose in the world.

The Noble Purpose Journey

> *"[E]very rule in the book can be broken, except one — be who you are, and become all you were meant to be."*
> — *Sidney J. Harris*

When you are connected to your Noble Purpose you gain a deeper knowledge of yourself and access a wider dimension of your gifts. Alignment of who you are in the world with your unique gifts allows you to make important contributions to others regardless of the scale. You are simultaneously freed and able to experience unbounded joy, vitality and a sense of accomplishment.

Wherever you are on the journey, discovering Noble Purpose is essentially about listening for this inner call. The fundamental notion of vocation is being called from within to use your unique gifts to serve others. Discovering your inner purpose may look formidable. It is not. Frequently this call to serve is very familiar, very obvious. It is an aspect of your life you have been flirting with since childhood, a completely original expression of your unique self.

Noble Purpose is not always a call to the extraordinary. More often than not it is the embrace of the ordinary, some basic urge or impulse, that makes you feel simply satisfied and good. It is not some holier-than-thou, remote or unobtainable end that is more about you feeling credible than authentically expressing what is essential to you.

Noble Purpose is fundamentally a matter of the heart. It is about your heart opening, feeling intimately united with others and your circumstances. Thus, Noble Purpose often arises out of the simple and ordinary that happens to be terribly important to you, that is fundamentally a quest of the heart. Theologian David Steindl-Rast asks, "What is it you tend to tackle with spontaneous mindfulness, so that without effort your whole heart is in it? … you find meaning in it — not a meaning you could spell out in words, but meaning in which you can rest" (*Gratefulness, the Heart of Prayer* 47).

If you do not immediately feel connected to your Noble Purpose, relax. Follow the pathways that this book provides and you will recognize the Noble Purpose within you. If you agonize over your Noble Purpose, you will have missed the point. Your Noble Purpose is already a creative force within you. Fulfilling your purpose entails, for many people, simply getting out of the way.

Why should you connect with your Noble Purpose if you have not already done so? Alternatively, if you know what your Noble Purpose is, but you are having trouble living it, why should you care? And if you are already living your Noble Purpose, how can you magnify the impact of your contribution? Even with a successful history of living your Noble Purpose, is there some new or different part of you that is seeking expression, giving birth to something new? This book provides perspective, wisdom and insights to help you find answers to these and other questions as you explore your own Noble Purpose, which may change over the course of your lifetime.

One last point: this book will not give you extraordinary Noble Purpose. This book points to an organic process wherein you engage your life and your world in a particular way. It describes the way to Noble Purpose, exemplified in the Noble Purpose Spiral. You and only you will discover or realize your Noble Purpose, and it is acquired not by reading words on paper but through contemplation and engagement in your life.

CHAPTER 2

The Bounded Self

> *What a long time it can take to become the person one has always been*
> *... before we discover our deep identity — the true self within every*
> *human being that is the seed of authentic vocation.*
>
> — *Parker Palmer*

Life is at times confronting and challenging. Each of us can expect to experience considerable anxiety over the course of our lifetime, especially in the workplace. Difficult childhood experiences and a variety of life circumstances can foster internal turmoil and worry. Such internalized experiences, often at an unconscious level, can impede our way in the world. We become hindered and stymied by any number of things, such as how we are perceived by others, fear of failing, feelings of dread associated with public performance or fear of risk.

The self that is immobilized because of such internalized feelings is identified here as the Bounded Self. We are not innately bounded. In fact, little children exhibit quite the opposite behavior, being fully unbounded and completely uninhibited.

Consider the pure essence and unlimited potential of a new infant. Most newborn babies are swaddled with unconditional compassion and love, thus the classic archetype: the Loved Child, who innocently and eagerly receives this love. The Loved Child accordingly trusts in the goodness of everything, including his or her own perfection and infinite potential and is fully consonant with his/her parents, surroundings and the contiguous universe. The admonition: "Be like little children" — the call to return to innocence, perfect faith, trust and the Essential Self, is an expression of this cherished archetype.

Using music as a metaphor, think of the Essential Self as being ensconced in harmony and perfect consonance. The capacity to see and partake in the world is fully present in this early stage of human development. This is the essential life force that is the birthright of every human being. This is where your Noble Purpose thrives and is accessible.

T. S. Eliot offers:

We shall not cease from exploration
And the end of all our exploring
Will be to arrive where we started
And know the place for the first time.

When you are powerfully connected with your Essential Self, as an adult engaged in the world, the miraculous can occur. The unattainable is suddenly within reach, allowing you to achieve extraordinary results that surprise and delight. Incredible capacities are unleashed when you are powerfully connected with your Essential Self. Your effectiveness far exceeds mere reliance on skills, education and conventional intelligence. The seemingly impossible becomes possible.

Painful and challenging things happen in childhood, often unintentional events caused by parents and loved ones or as a result of other life circumstances, resulting in a life-long indictment of ourselves. Wrapped around the Essential Self emerges a new layer, with its own tonal quality — the Fundamental Dissonance.

During my childhood, I remember feeling enveloped in love by wonderful parents and older brothers. And at some point, I recall learning that I would be going to school. I remember my family's encouragement and my anticipation about this new adventure.

?❧ *Fundamental Dissonance*

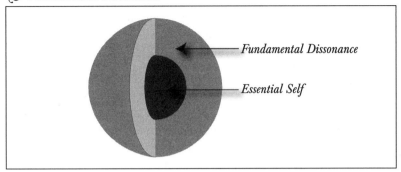

Fundamental Dissonance

Essential Self

I vividly recall waiting by myself at the end of my family's driveway with a shiny, new lunch box for my very first day of school. The huge yellow school bus, far bigger than I ever imagined, stopped just feet away from me on the country road where we lived. When the bus driver opened the door, I saw 60 laughing, screaming children. Every seat of the bus was taken, and no one offered to make room for me. Some of the children teased me about my lunch box, so much so that I became afraid, nauseated and physically ill.

At that moment I felt deeply that there must be something wrong with me. This concern about myself became a Fundamental Dissonance that cascaded through my life.

You, like most adults, had a Fundamental Dissonance, even if it resides in your unconsciousness now, that served to shape and influence your adult behavior. This Fundamental Dissonance displaces the Essential Self. Out of the dissonance comes self-diminishment and the experiences of fear, resignation, self-doubt, cynicism and/or resistance.

All great music contains dissonance and consonance. The dissonance is as necessary to satisfying music as is the consonance. Consonance is a combination of tones that have resolved — that is, that are in agreement. Dissonance is a combination of unresolved musical tones. In human affairs, you welcome the consonant — e.g., the feeling of satisfaction in having successfully accomplished a project. You tend to resist the dissonant — e.g., the feeling of frustration at having missed a deadline. Learning to allow for and embrace the dissonance can transform the dissonance.

In music, dissonance leads to resolution; it is a creative force of nature. Your dissonance and the related wounding may provoke discovery of your Noble Purpose. For example, you may help heal in others that which you seek to heal in yourself.

Nevertheless, dissonance in one's life is challenging and painful. Learning to live with, let alone embrace the dissonance, can be a life-long pursuit, thus the archetypal Injured Child. No matter how loving your environment and surroundings, difficult and sometimes painful things occur, like my childhood experience going to school. This causes you to compensate for the resulting behavior, in an attempt to protect yourself. This leads to the Bounded Self.

In response to a dissonant childhood experience, you begin to develop a hard, outer veneer, especially into adolescence, perfecting it throughout adulthood. This third layer serves as a boundary to protect you from the unpleasant dissonance operating within and around you. It serves as a boundary that encapsulates the pain of your dissonant, second circle, and, as a result of protecting yourself, there is an erosion of your life, vitality and capacity to access your Noble Purpose. Thus, the "Bounded" in Bounded Self.

The Bounded Self is expressed superficially in the form of your job title, possessions, how much money you make, social status, education, where you live, your viewpoints on politics and religion, your physical appearance — all of your physical, social, economic and psychological manifestations, quite removed and distinct from your Essential Self. None of these are you. Metaphorically, the song you sing becomes predictable and familiar. This changeless song becomes carved in stone, having a hard, impermeable facade. *You* become impermeable. You quite literally take on the characteristics attributed to this outer shell. And to some degree you feel protected from your dissonance, while simultaneously removed from your Essential Self.

The Bounded Self can become a force of remarkable accumulation. However, despite acquiring fame, possessions, wealth and a stellar reputation, the presence of the Bounded Self is not a path to peace and equanimity. It is

🐾 *Bounded Self*

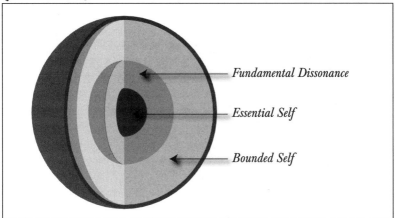

Fundamental Dissonance

Essential Self

Bounded Self

quite the opposite. The Bounded Self is constantly on edge, in a combative, defensive and protective posture, continually needing to safeguard your status, role and/or position in life. In defending your Bounded Self, masking your dissonance, you could completely miss the depth of person that is you, that is your Essential Self.

The cosmic joke is that you are already fully realized. You are whole, complete and perfect. The joyful, authentic energy that is you is your Essential Self. When you are free of neediness and the compulsion to protect, you have greater access to your Essential Self. Who you essentially are blossoms forth, life opens up bountifully and brilliantly.

When you rely on the more surface level, personal attributes of your outer, Bounded Self, you lack enthusiasm, freedom and inspiration to create and responsibly contribute to your world. Though not always conscious, the powerful dissonant forces within reverberate and manifest in your conduct. The outer two circles converge, causing you to gravitate to using power, control and manipulation to manage your environment and others. The pure potential and compassion of the Essential Self is displaced. You are separate, removed from your essence and others. You feel numb, empty and suppressed.

[handwritten annotation:] But even the shoe shine had to manipulated nerve his enviro? work & kids are part of such environment that must be managed

🐍 *The Descent to Your Essential Self*

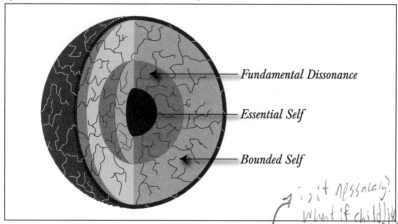

Fundamental Dissonance

Essential Self

Bounded Self

[handwritten margin note: is it nessasaly? What if childlike state so ho-]

Thus, a critical life quandary emerges. How do you return to your essence, to the buoyancy of your childlike state? The descent into your Essential Self requires that you enter into and embrace your Bounded Self, as well as your dissonant and painful experience.

There are ways and means to effectively embrace and work with all three dimensions of the three-circle model, but for now consider one way in which you penetrate through your hard outer veneer, reaching your Essential Self — the way of radical life transition. A critical life trauma, the loss of a loved one, a cataclysmic disease, a job loss, all create cracks in the outer veneer. Paradoxically, the challenge inherent in such a critical life change catapults you into your dissonance and provides access to your vulnerable, yet potent Essential Self. A Quaker proverb admonishes, "Blessed are the vulnerable, for they shall be broken, and being so, shall break open the heart of the Universe."

[handwritten margin note: forms neuron]

My early school trauma of not fitting in has followed me all of my life. I would strive to prove that I was more than OK in everything I did. My aim was to be the perfect son and student, making important contributions throughout my career by working harder and harder, embracing a work ethic that far exceeded the norm. My obsession to perform came more from compensating for my Fundamental Dissonance and less from my Essential Self.

In my early 50s, I realized I was working as hard as ever but feeling less and less satisfaction. In fact, I felt numb, purposeless, lifeless and adrift. And I got sick. Thankfully, I did not suffer a life-threatening illness, but it was severe enough to get my attention. During the recovery, I made a decision to take myself out of my work as a consultant — referring clients to colleagues and canceling speaking engagements. I began making daily retreats to the ocean, reflecting, journaling and meditating.

One day while visiting the ocean, I reflected and journaled about being awakened twice in my sleep the night before. In the first instance I could feel the food I ate earlier in the evening changing forms, moving slowly through my body, miraculously generating life-giving energy. In that twilight space, the remarkable chemical and biological processes within me, that I am unconscious of, became vividly alive. I was entranced by my body and how it nurtured me, moment by moment.

I reflected on the interdependent functioning of white and red blood cells, my heart, liver, kidneys, stomach and lungs, all working together in magical unity to maintain my health and wellbeing! This occurred seemingly independent of me, yet it was me. I was struck with how separate and removed I felt from these inner machinations.

Later, I had a second awareness inspired by the blazing full moon outside my window. I was conscious of its cycle occurring interdependently with all the planets and stars in the solar system and in perfect alignment with the great beyond of the infinite universe.

I could, ever so briefly, experience this cycle, with its movement and exquisite dance of light, mass and energy. In this twilight state I could actually attune myself to these planetary, astronomical movements in the heavens.

These cyclical images merged, and I felt strangely peaceful, at rest, in grace. I perceived some absolutely interconnected, precisely balanced relationship between the microscopic movements within me and the macroscopic movements outside and beyond me. How arrogant of me to assume that I could ever be outside or between these realities, certainly not beyond them. I was inextricably tied to and enveloped in these organic cycles of life.

I reflected on this while seated at the ocean. I knew everything was occurring cyclically, perfectly, with its own ebb and flow. Yet, memories of familiar dissonant voices from the past appeared before me — worry, fear and judgment. I wondered how worry and fear could exist in this magical web of perfection? How could I say fear and perfection in the same breath? What a cosmic joke that I would hold myself as imperfect, neglecting to notice the balance and perfection within and around me. How could I doubt the perfection of the universe? I experienced an expansive sense of freedom in realizing that everything is in its exact relationship, balanced and aligned, in perfect equanimity. There is nothing wrong with the universe and nothing wrong with me, I thought. I'm now awake to this truth.

My illness, healing and reflection at the ocean allowed me to reconnect with and reclaim my Essential Self. I simultaneously felt the pain and transcended the pain. My world was opened to me, as quite literally new doorways appeared — through the cracks — unleashing new possibilities, creating unforeseen passageways to accessing my Noble Purpose.

Given that wounds from childhood are part of the journey to adulthood, what can you do to reconnect with the magic of the unbounded, Essential Self? Reflecting on and connecting with your Fundamental Dissonance from childhood will assist you in your capacity to descend to your Essential Self. Chapter Seven provides a further exercise to help with this.

Connecting to the Essential Self — the Noble Purpose Spiral

> *It is better to sit by the temple and beg alms than do work you don't love ... Work is love made visible.*
>
> — *Khalil Gibran*

In Part II, you will be invited to actively engage the qualities of the Noble Purpose Spiral as the path to recovering your Essential Self. You will learn to cultivate the fertile ground from which to create and realize your purpose in the world. This book is less about guiding you to extraordinary Noble Purpose and more about helping you clear the way, to hear the Noble Purpose that is already alive and seeking expression within you, coming from your Essential Self.

𝔰 *Noble Purpose Spiral*

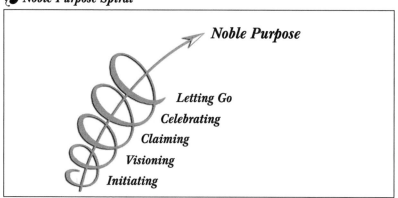

The Noble Purpose Spiral portrays an organic process, like the ebb and flow of the ocean. The qualities of the Spiral are highly interdependent considerations and not necessarily a linear progression. The Spiral is much more like the ocean than a machine. When you become sensitive to the fundamental aspects of extraordinary performance at work, as expressed in the Noble Purpose Spiral, you gain access to Noble Purpose and a life filled with incredible grace, satisfaction and joy.

The Six Qualities of the Noble Purpose Spiral

1. **Initiating** — The rite of passage to deep inner knowledge of, and trust in, the perfection of the universe, yourself, your circumstances and colleagues in the workplace.

2. **Visioning** — The revelation of imaginative new possibilities expressed through thought that manifests new reality.

3. **Claiming** — The manifestation of the contribution you envision for the world in tangible form and structure. Being your purpose.

4. **Celebrating** — The experience of profound gratitude and thanksgiving for the gifts of the universe.

5. **Letting Go** — The release of desperate clutching, power and control.

6. **Noble Purpose** — The generous giving and serving of others, bountifully reciprocated and inspiring high-level meaning and purpose in life and work, while taking care of yourself.

The six parts or qualities of the Noble Purpose Spiral are essentially pathways. You are invited to transverse these pathways to reach your Noble Purpose. These pathways lead you to a clearing away from the hustle and bustle of your life. It is a clearing within you. The clearing is a space wherein you come to terms with who you are — returning to your Essential Self. In this space, or clearing, you purge yourself of toxicities that interfere with experiencing your Noble Purpose. You release the old, dysfunctional, automatic response patterns and rigidities of the Bounded Self, gaining access to your Essential Self and the instinctive knowledge that allows you to move mountains.

The journey through the Spiral to Noble Purpose will at times be invigorating, enlivening and challenging. Trust this process. All that is necessary is that you authentically show up and put your full self forward. From this journey, you will have the potential of fostering a remarkable metamorphosis in your life and work.

is that even possible?

Part II

CHAPTER 3

Initiating

> *You are a child of the universe, no less than the trees and the stars; you*
> *have a right to be here. And whether or not it is clear to you, no doubt*
> *the universe is unfolding as it should.*
>
> — *Max Ehrmann*

**Initiating — Choosing the path of belonging and trust, knowing your
universe is perfectly unfolding.**

Initiating entails a rite of passage — movement through a catalytic space
wherein the nature of an entity or form is changed. There are many initiations
over the course of a life, but the sense of Initiating used here is of the elemental
initiation into a life that is inherently good. Those who undergo this rite of passage are fundamentally changed. David Steindl-Rast and Sharon Lebell affirm,
"… see with the eyes of trust that the cosmos is in fact prepared for us, like a
nurturing home. We have a right to feel at home here in the universe. It has been
marvelously created so as to be hospitable to human life … If we entrust ourselves to that fundamental sense of belonging to the universe, things go well,
and we can make some sense even out of the worst that happens to us" (*Music
of Silence* 110).

Initiating affirms the universe as an essentially fertile, nurturing place, a place of infinite goodness. This sense of Initiating is fused with knowing, at the deepest level of your being, that the universe is essentially good and that it is unfolding perfectly. The qualities of Initiating capture the life stance of the Essential Self and lay the groundwork for Noble Purpose.

This is not to say there are not destructive forces operating within the universe or incredibly difficult and challenging matters confronting communities, nations and the planet. According to the United Nations, for every 12 people living today, one is malnourished, including 160 million children under the age of five. This is intolerable. The world community carries on unconsciously in the face of this problem. This is not good news, and believing that the universe is perfectly unfolding seems completely naïve.

Yet, I have the opportunity to do something about this urgent problem. I can inform myself about the issue, learn what it takes and how much it costs to shift the circumstances that have allowed chronic hunger to persist and work with others to generate understanding that the world has the wherewithal to end hunger. That is good news.

Pain does exist, at a planetary and a personal level. Engaging the pain and confronting challenges and difficulties is an important implication of being on the path to Noble Purpose. We shall return to this theme at a personal level, in Chapter Seven on Letting Go.

Fully acknowledging that incredible pain and strife exists in the world, the foundation of the Spiral, Initiating, begins with the awareness that the universe is essentially benevolent and good. Out of knowing that you belong, and that you and others fully desire to make choices that create a better future, the world can be healed. Immersion in fear and resignation about others and yourself only inhibits and prevents the bold action that is necessary to change and heal.

However, Initiating, begins with the awareness that the universe is essentially benevolent, welcoming and nurturing. Closely related to this consciousness of welcoming and nurturing is the surrender into this awareness, experienced as belonging and trust.

Initiating as a rite of passage has us literally pass through a threshold. First we pass through a threshold within ourselves, that is, the inner dimension of Initiating that is characterized by a deep, internal trust that everything in the universe is just fine, that we are just fine. Secondly, we pass through the outer dimension, a threshold in our capacity to fuse, blend and merge with others out of our essential trust in others to do the right thing.

Inner Implications of Initiating

Everything that is a part of your world at this very moment is a result of your thinking and feeling. The opportunity to think and feel in a more conscientious, considerate way that contributes to others is part of the path to Noble Purpose.

You are the composite of many influences based upon your family of origin, your culture, your traditions, your education, etc. Many of these influences are useful and some are diminishing and not useful as they are influenced by your Fundamental Dissonance. However, you took on many of these influences unconsciously, as if they were true and unwavering, whether useful or diminishing. For example, as a child you may have been punished for speaking openly. You subconsciously believe that speaking openly results in being castigated, thus you have been cautious in expressing yourself throughout life — a direct result of your Fundamental Dissonance, leading to your Bounded Self.

These influences cause you to think and behave in inevitable ways. People and circumstances trigger predictable patterns of conduct. Like Pavlov's salivating dogs, you respond on cue, over and over again. This automatic response mechanism does not always engender feelings of trust and belonging in your life, in your relationships with work colleagues and, critically, within yourself.

Achieving your Noble Purpose requires consciousness and discernment, noticing what contributes and what detracts in terms of the greatest good you can produce (not just for the world but also for yourself). This requires personal change, and personal change is not easy.

Feeling victimized by life or work is a common symptom of the Bounded Self. Are you angry that you have been passed over for a particular job or promotion? Do you believe that you are smarter than your boss and should not be taking direction from him or her? This is predictable of a Bounded Self mentality. It requires greater rigor and discipline to embrace life as a good and remarkable gift than it does to feel victimized by it. But beware, the role of victim comes at great personal expense, not the least of which is undermining your contribution to the world. A powerful gift is available to you by simply knowing that you can always choose your current reality.

Isaiah, a 12-year-old caught up in the horror that was the Holocaust fell into deep despair during a hard winter in a Nazi concentration camp. His mother, father and sister had succumbed to slow and painful deaths by starvation at the hands of their captors. He knew that the chances of being rescued or even surviving much longer were slim. A sadistic guard beat him with a leather strap until he bled.

"All I knew was that I had to decide, once and for all, whether the horror I saw around me was the ultimate reality or whether the joy and tenderness I could still feel stirring inside me was the truth. I knew that they couldn't both be the truth," he recalled.

Isaiah contemplated this for months. "I wept over it, I wrestled with it, as Jacob must have wrestled with the angel for my life. I had to know, or I would drown in the darkness. For the first time, I started to pray. My prayer, which I began to repeat at every moment, was only four words: 'Show me the truth.' Nothing came. Not a single insight, not a single vision, no dream with any comforting angel."

But Isaiah went on praying, and then early one winter morning he heard a quiet voice say, "You must decide." For a week he reflected on this, wondering "... what could the voice mean? How could I, a child, decide the truth of the universe?" Then, one morning, Isaiah awoke thinking about his mother, his cat at home, and the flowers and vegetables in their kitchen garden. Suddenly, he knew what he had to do as he grasped what was at the bottom of his heart — "I choose Love! I choose Love! I choose Love!"

And then Isaiah opened his eyes and saw "… a sun not of this world had come out and was blazing glory all around me … The guard I hated … came out of another building … He didn't see me, but I saw him and — this was the miracle — I felt no fear at all, and no hatred, only a burning pity that scalded my eyes with tears … the Thing in me that was crying was stronger than anything or anyone I had ever encountered. It … felt like a calm column of fire that nothing could put out" (Harvey 3-8).

The rite of passage leading to the perfection of the universe is not always filled with the same light and beauty that characterizes that perfection. Quite the opposite is sometimes true, as the path may be dense with shadow and dread. Isaiah is a case in point. Excruciating pain may prompt the passing, fostering the initiation. Isaiah cracked open, making the deep descent to the Essential Self and the awareness of the fundamental goodness of the universe. The path to Initiating is often paradoxical — the loss of a job, the death of a loved one and the ensuing pain from life's calamities may be catalytic to spawning new Noble Purpose within you.

As Max Ehrmann affirms, "… the universe is unfolding as it should." There is no insufficiency, no lack, nothing is missing within you. And nothing is missing in the universe. Every resource, person, circumstance is readily available to help you realize the Noble Purpose that inspires you.

In fact, everyone has extraordinary Noble Purpose, it lies within the Essential Self, and everyone has the wherewithal to realize his or her Noble Purpose. Out of this knowing about the perfection of life you are better able to explore and discover your Noble Purpose.

This knowing leads to a deep sense of trust. Initiating is the rite of passage to trusting in yourself, in others and trusting that Noble Purpose is your birthright. This rite of passage is closely coupled with trust that all is well, feeling that you belong, that the universe is your home and it is a safe and supportive place. This sense of belonging provides a resilient platform for vast creativity and living a life of Noble Purpose.

David Steindl-Rast defines spirituality as deep belonging and connection. Thus, Initiating is a deeply spiritual consideration at the heart of discovering and realizing Noble Purpose. You know that you have access to an exquisite and perfectly unfolding series of impulses, urges and capacities that can be brought to bear on the realization of your Noble Purpose.

Outer Implications of Initiating

Such belonging fosters deeper, broader relationships with others as you experience, viscerally, your connection with all others in the world. You actively seek out and nurture connections and relationships with others, reconnecting to your Essential Self and laying the foundation for you to discover your Noble Purpose.

When you live with such fervent trust within yourself, it translates into your relationships with others and into the outer world. You gain others' great respect, provide them enormous space to be who they are, and, as a result, you foster powerful relationships within teams and organizations.

Experience reveals that not much is possible without powerful Initiating — without first establishing a background of relationships with co-workers. Colleagues will find it advantageous to discover connections, relationships and ways to support each other. If the quality of relationships between co-workers is diminished, it is useful to foster it early in the process of the team. Realize that strong, trusting relationships with colleagues begin with a resilient inner regard for yourself, your perfection and the perfection of the universe.

How to Achieve Trust in the Essential Goodness of Life

How can I create this positive stance of achieving trust and belonging? An effective way to advance this thinking is to release relentless evaluation and obsessive worry. Evaluation and its associated worry is the primary impediment to noticing, let alone realizing, Noble Purpose.

Suspending evaluation of others and, essentially, evaluation of yourself is a critical challenge of this book. This suspension is very difficult because of years of conditioning. The single greatest discipline that you can cultivate to foster Noble Purpose is releasing evaluation and the related worry fostered by the Bounded Self.

Often, our predisposition is to assign the dissonance we feel to someone or something else. We quickly jump to the conclusion that some external person or circumstance is causing our pain. This is a sure way to undermine our Noble Purpose. Noble Purpose calls us to a higher level of integrity — one where we take responsibility for our pain, acknowledging that we always have a choice. For example, in the case of the child who was punished for speaking openly, becoming conscious of the pain in being reprimanded and the resulting pattern of guarded communications as an adult allows you to take responsibility, suspend evaluation and choose instead to be fully self-expressive in the future.

Thus, learn to embrace your dissonance, without evaluating, without laying blame on something, someone or even yourself. An important Initiating capacity is to release the thought that others have anything to do with what you are feeling. You must take responsibility for yourself.

Taking responsibility will lead to an important lesson. "What is this situation teaching me? What do I need to learn from this difficult interaction?" In this way, you return yourself to the perfection in life and simultaneously promote your Noble Purpose.

The notion of Initiating and the trust in the essential goodness of life requires a suspension of all evaluation and faith that everything in the universe is perfectly unfolding. The paradox at this unfolding is that you have free will and that you may choose consistently with that perfection and you may not. As the opposite of faith is doubt, Initiating is free of doubt. Instead, it is a doorway to perfect equanimity and peace.

When you are in touch with life's essential goodness, your energy is released and your world expands radically. You fully live in this moment, not in the past, not in the future. This invocation suggests the pathway necessary to fully live in the now, moment by moment.

When you hold the world, others or yourself in doubt, your energy is depleted. It is used up, and you live out of your past or are preoccupied with the future as a substitute for the exquisite present. You surrender to the involuntary flow of past- or future-based doubts from your relentless, unremitting logical mind. You become an inert, unmoving mass, disengaged and disempowered. You wither and dry up.

This depletion runs rampant in organizations. Sometimes it runs rampant in your life. But you have a choice. You can accept the perfection of the universe and everything in it, including yourself, or you can succumb to a doubt-filled, depleted existence.

It is quite simple. You are the right person at the right time given the current state of your relationships, family, community, planet and, most importantly, your current or evolving service in the world. The challenge is awakening to this reality. The essential aspects of Initiating follow:

Initiating schema:

1. Choose to release all evaluation of yourself, others and/or circumstances and related worry.

2. Become conscious of gifts, resources and blessings in your life.

3. Embrace learning from dissonance in your life/work.

4. Acknowledge and affirm perfection in your life/work, trusting that nothing is missing in your universe.

Initiating in Your Daily Routine

Choose one of the following processes for integrating Initiating into your daily routine. For maximum benefit, it is recommended that you create an affirmation statement and perform either the anchoring activity, body exercise, ritual, artistic expression, journal writing or aesthetic appreciation, described as follows.

Affirmation

Create an affirmation that emphasizes and/or strengthens a particular implication of this chapter that would assist you in your journey to Noble Purpose. Write the affirmation on an index card or a piece of paper and carry it with you today. Repeat the affirmation several times before lunch, before ending your workday and before retiring in the evening.

For example, try this affirmation: "I experience the universe as benevolent, completely supporting my well-being and life journey." Alternatively, focusing on what you are not, may be more powerful for some people: "I experience no insufficiency, no lack, nothing is missing within me and nothing is missing in my universe. I powerfully generate in the world."

Anchoring Activity

How do you learn to trust the essential goodness of life? You do this in two ways: first by releasing all evaluative and worrisome thoughts and second by allowing yourself the exquisite gift of experiencing the perfection in your moment-by-moment existence.

Scan your thoughts today, noticing the formation of a worried or troubled thought. Stop immediately at the first sign and work with that thought by performing the following steps.

1. For a minute or so, fully experience the worry and/or dissonance regarding this situation. Let it in. Feel it. Don't resist it. What you resist persists and resistance obscures Noble Purpose.

2. Return yourself to a place of calm and serenity and become aware of your breath, slowly inhaling and exhaling; be aware of the chair or floor that is supporting you; notice any tightness in your body and release it.

3. And now return yourself to life's perfection, releasing any negative, evaluative and/or worried thoughts.

4. Acknowledge that the dissonance you experienced is within you and continue to feel it if it persists, embracing it as your dissonance, taking full responsibility for it.

5. Release making something, someone or yourself responsible for your experience of dissonance. Repeat the following: "I release (something, someone or yourself) as being the cause of my experience of dissonance."

6. Stay alert to the here and now, savoring that life is perfectly unfolding, considering the lesson that this situation provides you.

7. Notice your interior experience. Record what you notice in your journal or notebook.

Body Exercise

Take 10-15 minutes to sit in quiet, releasing your thoughts with eyes closed. Consider the following reflection, paying particular attention to a body sensation.

Consider a time in your childhood when you were most in awe of the perfection of the universe. Upon identifying such a time, notice where in your body you felt this satisfaction and pleasure. Was it an experience of your heart opening? Do you remember having a rapid and increased pulse or a feeling of joy and rapture above your eyes? Scan your body and be aware of where in your body you most sensed that pleasure. Stay mindful of that place and that feeling, returning to it when circumstances are challenging or stressful.

Ritual

Where do you feel most at peace and attuned with the world around you? In a special room in your home? A place of worship? In nature? Consciously go to that place and allow yourself to feel a deep connection with the blessings of your life. If you are not physically able to go to that place, close your eyes and visualize being there, sharing the fullness of your experience of connection with everyone and everything.

Artistic Expression

Recall a time when you felt most attuned to the goodness of life. Find something in nature, at work or elsewhere that signifies that perfection in the universe and everything in it. Position what you find in a highly visible place in your home or office so that you can see it. If possible, mount or hang it so as to create distinction for it in your home/office. If it is possible to adorn or decorate this symbol with color (paper, paint/ink, ribbon, etc.) proceed to embellish your symbol, fashioning it into your own art form.

Journaling Activity

Identify people from your childhood through the present who live/lived life as if the universe is innately good and wonderful. These people may be living or dead. They may be people who were, or are still, a part of your immediate circle of friends and colleagues, or they may be people you admire from afar, for example, someone famous whom you know only through reading or school. For each person you identify, reflect in your journal on what precisely he or she said or did that reinforced the perfection of the universe and how they affected your world view.

Rekindling Awareness for Initiating Through Aesthetic Appreciation

There are many ways to rekindle your awareness for an important idea or thought, changing how you think or feel about some reality in your life/work.

Three different forms of aesthetic appreciation are described below, and you may wish to use one or more to rekindle the ideas expressed in this chapter on Initiating. The aesthetic forms include music, poetry and painting. These are only recommendations. You would be well-served to reflect on various forms of aesthetic expression, choosing something you feel drawn to, and then using it to help embed the reality of Initiating in your consciousness.

Music — Find a favorite piece of music that exemplifies Initiating in the Noble Purpose Spiral and listen to it throughout the day, allowing the lyric or melody to enter your psyche, reinforcing the qualities associated with Initiating. Record the music on a cassette tape or CD and listen to it on your way to work, at work if at all possible and/or at home each day.

Songs, like John Denver's *Sunshine on My Shoulders*, incorporate many of the qualities associated with Initiating in their lyrics: "Sunshine on my shoulders makes me happy; Sunshine in my eyes can make me cry," as the song goes. "Sunshine on the water looks so lovely; Sunshine almost always makes me high."

Poetry — Be aware of your favorite poems, and choose one that contains the elements of Initiating as expressed in the Noble Purpose Spiral. Record the poem on an index card or a small piece of paper and place it in your pocket. Periodically, recite the poem to yourself and to significant others in your life throughout the day.

For example, see this excerpt of e.e. cummings' poem of thanksgiving:

> *i thank you God for most this amazing*
> *day; for the leaping greenly spirits of trees*
> *and a blue true dream of sky; and for everything*
> *which is natural which is infinite which is yes*
>
> *... now the ears of my ears are awake and*
> *now the eyes of my eyes are opened*

Painting — Consider your favorite paintings and choose a painting that evokes the quality of Initiating for you. Notice how the use of color, texture, shape and form resonate with you and this quality of the Noble Purpose Spiral. Place the painting, photo or other rendering of the painting, in full view so that you can connect with it as you go through the day. If it is inconvenient to take it to work with you, then place it in a conspicuous place in your home, allowing it to provoke in you the qualities associated with Initiating. If it is possible to capture the image of this favorite painting electronically, place it as wallpaper in your personal computer so that it greets you throughout the day.

CHAPTER 4

Visioning

> *Not much happens without a dream. And for something great to happen, there must be a great dream. Much more than a dreamer is required to bring it to reality; but the dream must be there first.*
>
> *— Robert Greenleaf*

Visioning — Discovering your passion and purpose, visualizing it in the world.

Noble Purpose is not "out there," it resides within your Essential Self, alive and well within you, waiting to be discovered. Visioning is the capacity to bring Noble Purpose to light.

Attempting to leap frog to Visioning without first successfully completing the rites of passage associated with Initiating, will bear little fruit. When you carry the worries of the world or are consumed by self-evaluation, the evaluation of others or circumstances characteristic of the Bounded Self, you will generate far too much inner static to sense your Noble Purpose.

For example, do you ever catch yourself saying things like this to yourself?

- "I've made too many wrong decisions in my life, and it is too late to do anything about it now."

- "I can't possibly give up my current job, even though I hate it, to do something different."
- "I have a family to support and I can't just give up my salary and retirement benefits to follow a dream."
- "What I have is as good as it gets. I don't want to make waves and lose everything I have."

Coming from these resigned and cynical points of view, the odds of your revealing, let alone realizing, Noble Purpose are greatly diminished. If your view is optimistic about the essential goodness of life, you will want to deepen the exploration, revealing what excites and inspires you.

Revealing the Inner Source of Your Energy

Visioning is largely about energy and developing a facility at working with the energy deep within you. Noble Purpose resides at the source of your innermost energy, which is present in your Essential Self.

Consider how a common household toaster works. The external manifestations of the toaster include the case, heating elements, bell, springs and thermostat. This is the form and structure of the toaster. But it is all for naught without energy, specifically electricity, the animating force that allows the toaster to function. Similarly, your fully manifested Noble Purpose may take on a physical form, being composed of analogous springs and thermostats, but critically, at the heart of your Noble Purpose lies energy, that which animates you.

Begin first by considering the process for revealing and getting in touch with the source of your energy, then how you access and use this energy. A key aspect of this process of revealing your energy is listening more deeply and reflectively, to your inner voice, to your intuition, at this time in your life.

Animation Process — Use the following process to become attuned to your Essential Self's deep reservoir of energy which is necessary to the animation of your Noble Purpose. There are three parts to this process:

1. Brainstorming the sources of your passion.

2. Journaling about the implications of your brainstorming ideas.

3. Reflecting on the synergy of those implications with the purpose of discerning glimpses of your Noble Purpose.

The process is designed to unearth a variety of impulses and urgings that might help you better envision aspects of your Noble Purpose.

1. Begin by brainstorming five lists:

a. Consider first your childhood experiences. Your childhood memories are a particularly rich source of information about the penchant of your Essential Self, uncontaminated by the protection and rigidity of the Bounded Self that you crafted through adolescence and later adulthood. In your journal or on notepaper, record your earliest childhood hopes and dreams in the following four categories:

- Things you liked to do.
- Possessions you liked to have.
- Adventures you liked to take.
- Fantasies you liked to experience.

Record as many thoughts, ideas or illustrations as you can, merely listing the ideas without further elaboration in each category. Place each idea or thought to the extreme left hand side of the page, leaving a line or two between each item.

On the right side of this page, indicate in one or two words the feelings associated with these childhood memories.

b. Now consider your current experience as an adult. In your journal or on notepaper, record your current hopes and dreams for the same four categories.

- Things you would like to do (note especially current hobbies or hobbies you would like to cultivate).
- Possessions you would like to have (note physical or material things that excite and energize you, especially at a vocational level).
- Adventures you would like to take (note exciting new travel plans or expeditions).

♦ Fantasy experiences you would like to experience (note outrageous things you might do or be).

Note as many thoughts, ideas or illustrations as you can think of, merely listing the ideas without further elaboration, in each of these four categories. Place each idea or thought to the extreme left hand side of the page, leaving a line or two between each item. On the right side of this page, indicate in one or two words the feelings associated with having these impulses and urges.

c. In your journal or on notepaper, list as many of your favorite movies and books as you can recall from throughout your life. List the movies or books, without further elaboration, to the extreme left hand side of the page, leaving a line or two between each item.

After doing so, jot down a few words on the right side of the page, identifying the hero or heroine or the story line of each book or movie that you found so memorable and why. When finished, go on to the next part of this process.

d. Identify "mountaintop experiences" from throughout your life when you felt a life-changing, transcendent, ecstatic experience. They may be as simple as viewing a sunrise in the early morning or receiving a warm embrace from a family member. Scan for such remarkable experiences and list them, without further elaboration, to the extreme left hand side of the page, leaving a line or two between each item. On the right side of the page indicate feelings and body sensations that these experiences provoke. Once you are finished, go on to the next part of this process.

e. Make a list of your greatest accomplishments. Which accomplishment gives you the greatest pride? List as many accomplishments as you can without elaboration on the extreme left-hand side of the page, leaving a line or two between each.

Note on the right side of the page what contribution is embedded within each accomplishment. Name your gifts in just a few words, identifying them with each accomplishment. When finished, go on to the second part of this process.

2. Review all five lists, underlining those items on your lists that create unusual energy for you at this time in your life. After selecting those items, return to your journal or notepaper and reflect on the interdependencies that you see among these seemingly disparate items, becoming aware of how the energy you feel relates to these items and exemplifies your spiritual core or Essential Self. Then proceed to the third and final part of this process.

3. In your journal or on notepaper, begin to discern what the myriad of images and impulses from the previous parts of this process suggest about your Noble Purpose. What inspires you? Listen. Quietly discern. As in the toaster metaphor, what animates you? What is the source of that animation? Picture or envision your response through drawing or written reflections and indicate how you might live your Noble Purpose and how it might enliven you. Reflect on how you might better respect and honor your personal uniqueness. Once you have completed all of these steps, what concretely can you now say about your Noble Purpose?

Visioning as Accessing and Using Your Energy

Great Visioning reveals Noble Purpose or glimpses of Noble Purpose. Revealing this energy is one thing but accessing and using this energy is quite another. Accessing this animating force is often a matter of getting out of the way — getting out of your own way — quieting your mind, releasing cynical inner voices and the rigidities of your Bounded Self. You must allow what animates you to move you, potentially leading to a remarkable sense of possibility. Out of that freedom and possibility, miracles can occur. There is no separating you from the animating force, you become what Mihaly Csikszentmihalyi calls "Flow" (*Flow* 1-8).

Inspired Visioning may be prompted by an obstacle or challenge. Trust that the challenge is a "gift," awakening you to something new. Stay present to the obstacle or challenge; don't resist it. Notice that resisting only pulls you into a deeper sleep and further boundedness. Embrace the obstacle or challenge. Let it in, fully. Allow it to teach you, generating new visionary possibilities that transcend this current obstacle.

Physicists tell us that at the subatomic level we are fundamentally fluctuations or waves of subtle energy. These fluctuations of energy, in the form of thoughts (which are in themselves brain waves) manifest Noble Purpose in the world. There is a particular kind of thought that is fused with powerful energy. This is the kind that takes the form of a potent, heart-felt yearning or craving that emanates from your Essential Self. Such yearning or craving is inherently more fused with energy than ordinary thought — such as a thought that is static and more from our head than our heart (see particularly Hawkins' *Power vs. Force, The Hidden Determinants of Human Behavior*, 1995).

Thought that is of this higher frequency of energy, that is a yearning or thirsting tied to your Noble Purpose, is infinitely creative. It changes the world. Breakthrough-results live in the domain of this yearning to fundamentally contribute and serve. This particular kind of thought invokes a spectrum of sensory responses and it changes life materially.

The transformation of this yearning or thirsting into intention greatly animates the potential for creation in the world. Powerful intention, grounded in Noble Purpose, is yet a higher frequency of energy than thirsting, that is, something you hope for or think would be nice to have. Intention has within it the seeds of the manifestation of Noble Purpose.

Powerful intention demonstrates a basic law of the universe — that everything is energy and, further, that thought harnesses energy. Out of clear intention comes powerful attention on what needs to be accomplished. We will explain claiming of actions to realize Noble Purpose in the next chapter.

Outer Dimension of Visioning

Visioning Noble Purpose in a work environment with members of your team or organization follows precisely these same approaches to revealing, accessing and using energy. It becomes a bit more complex as the group works to align personal and organizational Noble Purpose. And with this exploration and realization of organizational Noble Purpose, we enter into the outer dimensions of Visioning.

Great Visioning in organizations manifests itself through strong team and organizational relationships. It leads to organizational and team identity and values and is the precursor to revealing and accessing collective Noble Purpose. Team members recognize the synergy of possibilities that transcend any one individual, generating the richest possible vision of contribution to customers.

Individuals function synergistically to provoke the big picture. They are present to the core values, beliefs and Noble Purpose of the group — such that it is alive and experienced viscerally by all members of the group.

Great Visioning whether at the inner level, individual level or the team/organization level is essentially about effectively using energy to access and realize our potential for good. Consider these simple steps that capture the essence of Visioning.

Visioning schema:

1. Become conscious of sources of energy or passion, from activities, projects or interests in your life/work.

2. Discern images/urgings that are related to your source of energy that inspire you.

3. Visualize your purpose/inner call to serve.

Applying Visioning in Your Daily Routine

Choose one of the following processes for integrating Visioning into your daily routine. For maximum benefit, it is recommended that you create an affirmation and complete either the anchoring activity, body exercise, ritual, artistic expression, journal writing or aesthetic appreciation, described as follows.

Affirmation

Create an affirmation that emphasizes and/or strengthens a particular implication of this chapter that would assist you in your journey to Noble Purpose. Write the affirmation on an index card or a piece of paper and carry it with you today. Repeat the affirmation several times before lunch, before ending your workday and before retiring in the evening.

For example, "I attract everything I need — information, understanding and perspective — necessary to envision my extraordinary Noble Purpose."

Anchoring Activity

How do you access your Noble Purpose? It requires creating a space for it to show up. This is key to Visioning. Creating that space requires openness to everything around you. Take time to reflect on the following points:

- Develop the capacity to "listen" for subtle messages, i.e., inner urgings regarding the vision of your Noble Purpose.

- Everyone possesses some Noble Purpose, some inner sensibility that is seeking expression in the world.

- Noble Purpose is not remote — it is living in and through you, even if dormant. It is an elemental part of you. Noble Purpose exists in you as a wave exists in the ocean. It is there for you to reveal as an intention.

- The messages that will guide you to Noble Purpose lie within you and within your environment. In the morning, during midday and once before retiring, discern and listen carefully to what others are telling you, what nature is telling you and what your body tells you about your vision.

Body Exercise

Take 10-15 minutes of quiet time, releasing your thoughts, and closing your eyes. Consider the following reflection, paying attention to any sensations you might have in your body.

At the heart of great Visioning is working with energy. Energy exists throughout your body. Begin with your hands — do you feel energy tingling in your hands? Place your hands several inches apart and notice the field of energy between your palms and fingers of both hands. Begin, slowly at first, moving your hands back and forth, one to two inches. Feel the energy. Move your hands in a circular movement. Do you notice the energy changing? How does it change? Now move your hands four to six inches apart and notice how the energy changes. Then move your hands nine to 12 inches apart and begin to move your hands back and forth, six inches or so. What sensation do you feel? Whenever you are troubled or experience any anxiety about your Noble Purpose pay attention to your hands and re-experience the energy that is always present within you.

Ritual

Visioning is significantly about revealing or bringing your Noble Purpose into the light. This evening, find a quiet corner in your home, away from family and significant others, in a darkened space and light a candle — or, better yet, light several candles. As you light your candles, hold the thought of the full-bodied expression of your Noble Purpose in the world. See the magnificence of your creation. Sit quietly in the light of candles and let in, fully, the light from the candles and the light of your Noble Purpose.

Artistic Expression

Dwell on your success in bringing extraordinary Noble Purpose to the world. Notice what you feel. Reflect on a color, a shape and/or images that you associate with that feeling. Don't over-analyze. Allow the colors and images to emerge and then, on a piece of paper, sketch/draw/paint the shape, image and/or colors that come to mind. Create a "credo" or a guiding principle that points the way to fulfilling your Noble Purpose and record it on your rendering.

Journaling Activity

Record five things that would be really remarkable if they occurred over the next six months, whether related or unrelated to your Noble Purpose. Allow yourself to really dream. Don't think small; allow yourself the exquisite pleasure of knowing that these things will occur. Notice how you feel about realizing these five wishes. On your calendar, look out exactly six months from today's date and make a notation so as to return to this place in your journal (mark the page in the journal with a Post-it note or in some other way so that you can find it). Six months from now record in your journal all feelings/experience related to your wish list.

Rekindling Awareness for Visioning Through Aesthetic Appreciation

There are many ways to rekindle your awareness for an important idea or thought, changing how you think or feel about some reality in your life/work. Three different forms of aesthetic expression are described below, you may wish to use one or more to rekindle the ideas expressed in this chapter on Visioning. The aesthetic forms include music, poetry and painting. These are only recommendations. You would be well-served to reflect on various forms of aesthetic expression, choosing something you feel drawn to, and then using it to help embed the reality of Visioning in your consciousness.

Music — Find a favorite piece of music that exemplifies Visioning in the Noble Purpose Spiral and listen to it throughout the day, allowing the lyric or melody to enter your psyche, reinforcing the qualities associated with Visioning. Listen to the music on your drive to work, at work if possible and/or at home at the end of the day.

Morning Has Broken is a song that is infused with the qualities associated with Visioning: "Morning has broken, like the first morning; Blackbird has spoken, like the first bird; Praise for the singing, praise for the morning."

Poetry — Of your favorite poems, choose one that contains elements of Visioning as expressed in the Noble Purpose Spiral. Record the poem on an index card or a small piece of paper and place it in your pocket. Periodically throughout the day, find the poem and recite it to yourself and to significant others in your life. For example, "Easter Morning in Wales" is a poem by David Whyte that embodies the essential ideas of Visioning. Here is a brief excerpt:

I have woken from the sleep of ages and I am not sure
if I am really seeing, or dreaming,
or simply astonished
walking toward sunrise
to have stumbled into the garden
where the stone was rolled from the tomb of longing.

Painting — Consider your favorite paintings and choose one that evokes the quality of Visioning for you. Notice how the use of color, texture, shape and form resonate within you and this quality of the Noble Purpose Spiral. Place the painting or a photo or other rendering of the painting in full view so that you can connect with it as you go through the day. If it is inconvenient to bring it to work with you, then place it in a conspicuous place in your home, allowing it to provoke in you the qualities associated with Visioning. If it is possible to capture the image of this favorite painting electronically, save it as wallpaper on your personal computer so that it greets you throughout the day.

CHAPTER 5

Claiming

*What's the one thing I'm not doing right now that if I were, would
make the biggest difference?*

— *Stephen Covey*

Claiming — Being accountable and responsible; manifesting your vision.

The cornerstone of great Claiming, fulfilling your Noble Purpose, is not the
popular-culture notion of long hours, sweat, pain and toil or being the "good
soldier." Rather, it is embodying your unique purpose, with ease, grace and
equanimity while soundly grounded in your Essential Self.

Claiming is essentially about doing, keeping your word and getting the job
done. Taken alone, Claiming is insufficient. Great Claiming fuses and blends
with all of the qualities of the Noble Purpose Spiral. We are far more than human
"doers," we are more vast, richer, deeper and wider. We are fully human beings.

If Initiating catapults us beyond insufficiency and scarcity, transcending
doubt, worry and mistrust of people and circumstances, then Claiming is that
transforming agent that creates action and results in the world.

Jennifer, a young woman employed in a Fortune 100 telecommunications
company, desperately wanted to leave her job because she didn't fit in.

Fortunately, she resisted and instead found her place by setting a high course, changing the face of her corporation. Out of her decision to stay and her considerable contribution, she rose from the position of secretary to project manager and through a series of appointments, to director of organization development for the Asia Pacific division. She shares:

> *At age 30 I was employed in a major telecommunications company. I was resigned about my work, feeling that I didn't matter, nor did my co-workers. I confided to a friend that I wanted to leave the company. She asked if I'd be interested in attending a week-long program probing the deeper implications of work and finding the spirit in team and organization.*
>
> *Little did I know the impact of my accepting that invitation. There are moments in time when I know there is something at work greater than any human could devise. Call it alignment, divine intervention, serendipity, synchronicity — dumb luck — whatever you wish, but whatever you call it the importance of its occurrence doesn't change. It simply happens and, if you're sufficiently awake, you notice it when it does.*
>
> *As a result of this program and my willingness to be vulnerable about challenges I experienced at that time, I changed. I became a new woman — amazingly, rapidly, in the blink of an eye — transformed. Or rather, I became more myself, someone who would take risks unparalleled in my organization, in my universe. I never intended to become that woman, or to change that day. It just happened, like the sun rising — with such ultimate certainty that I was unsure of exactly what had just altered.*
>
> *While I had an intention to become a champion for change in my company I was confronted with the claim that my vision was antithetical to my current reality. Realizing that I would need to be in a position that would provide a platform for the change I wished to make, I sought the support of colleagues in the development of a plan to secure a new position within the company. I positioned myself to apply for, and was then accepted as, an internal organization development consultant.*

I felt as if I crossed an internal threshold to a doorway formerly blocked years and years before. I opened my heart to any who would listen and looked for those who were capable of listening.

I spoke with every coworker who would take the time, to every team leader who had the slightest interest in new ways for teams to work together more humanely, with greater spirit. I was amazed. My high-tech colleagues, trained in the best colleges and universities, brilliant and alert, opened, listened and responded with interest. Within a matter of months 10, then 20, 30, 40 colleagues: team leaders, engineers, secretaries stepped forward. They agreed to be a part of a cadre of people who would become competent in and deliver this new form of team development. At the end of one year, nearly half of the employees of my division had participated.

I began, almost unknowingly, a journey of self-discovery and self-awareness that was challenging and difficult, a demanding spiritual path. Eventually, life's challenges and victories were of little consequence; what mattered was how the people were, the individual lives — of those that I served and honestly realizing that I served all human beings I encountered each day. I moved to larger projects and roles that increased the number of people and organizations I touched. In four years I became a senior leader in the Asia Pacific division of my company — caring for and supporting over 1,000 people. Today, my journey begins anew with each step, each opening of my heart, every risk, each day and with every passing year.

Being Your Purpose: Inner Level

Jennifer was vulnerable enough to descend into and share from her Essential Self. The journey required boldness. She possessed such boldness, trusting in the essential goodness of herself, others and the universe. She held a vision and claimed actions that would allow her to minimize the restraints and maximize her capacity to lovingly bring herself to each person and situation she encountered.

Jennifer demonstrated Claiming that originated from her inner strength and confidence. She wedded inner peace and confidence with laser-like action and productivity. Her performance occurred easily, effortlessly, without drama or pain. This is the zone of inspired Claiming.

Notice when Claiming is not inspired, when what you are doing becomes obsessive, compulsive and mindless. How frequently do you try to get somewhere quicker, faster, more persistently — some place other than where you actually are? Is your life just a means to arriving somewhere, an ongoing series of somewheres, a means to an end?

When you are in the flow of inspired Claiming you accomplish more than you ever imagined and you do it with less energy, without force, manipulation or control. Results occur naturally, with ease. At the core is a powerful intention that leads to effective Claiming.

Critical to great Claiming is that you are ready for it. With Claiming you assert, "I am able." "I make a difference in the world." Claiming, at the inner level, is knowing that you are critical to the fulfillment of your Noble Purpose.

Structure is important to Claiming; not the superfluous order and structure of excessive regimentation, but order and structure that allows you to brilliantly deliver extraordinary Noble Purpose. Such order and structure frees you to set things in motion such that they occur powerfully in the world — things like money, time, resources (human and material) and, most importantly, process.

Achieving your Noble Purpose, revealed through Visioning, requires you to break down the components of your mission into bite-sized action steps. Please proceed to Appendix A for a useful process that invites you to formulate action steps related to your Noble Purpose. The approach offered is based upon a well-known organization theory developed by Kurt Lewin.

Being Your Purpose: Outer Level

The outer dimension of Claiming is the alignment with your team or colleagues on goals and roles that lead to extraordinary Noble Purpose, leaving you and your colleagues in action, sustaining you and them in the achievement of the team's aims. In turn, the team becomes its purpose, fulfilling its roles and goals, bringing desired tangible results into the world.

Claiming, inspired action in the world, arises out of a solid background of relationships with colleagues (Initiating) and powerful intentions (Visioning). Thought that is so essential in Visioning manifests tangible results in the world through Claiming.

When we think of work, we most often think of Claiming. It is the overt expression of the outer dimension of work performed in the world. And, in many organizations, it exists as a preoccupation with establishing goals and roles, task accountabilities and milestones. If we are preoccupied with Claiming, then our work is incomplete, often limp and ineffectual, devoid of Noble Purpose and separate from critical Initiating and Visioning and the other qualities of the Noble Purpose Spiral.

With great Claiming, the team can reach agreement on action steps and timelines, experience ownership and solidarity for their work and do all of this in a place of self-confidence and equanimity.

Threats to Claiming

There are three forces that undermine great Claiming. Be mindful of how they can sabotage you in experiencing your Noble Purpose:

a. Power and control.

b. Fixation on results.

c. Looking good.

Each of these undermining considerations is motivated by fear of your Fundamental Dissonance, making you feel you are not enough, they are not enough, it is not enough. Fear undermines Noble Purpose and is the antithesis of trust in the inherent goodness and rightness of people and circumstances of Initiating.

Seeking power and control through the Bounded Self contaminates Noble Purpose — it is no longer noble and it undermines thought that is generative.

The use of power and control is motivated by not feeling enough, not trusting, not being in harmony with one's Essential Self. Such forced achievement of your intended contribution is self-defeating. As reflected in Jennifer's story, Noble Purpose comes most profoundly with surrender into the heart-felt intention to serve.

Claiming is not rigidly fixated on the result. It does not clutch or fiercely cling to achieving your purpose. It is not desperately attached to the outcome. In releasing this fixation on results and holding on, at all expense, comes a remarkable freedom to generate bountifully.

Similarly, the Bounded Self's preoccupation with looking good diminishes and obscures Noble Purpose. Noble Purpose is not about being loved, admired or affirmed by others. Claiming is not about seeking nobility. It is not about title, role, who you work for or how much money you make. These are impediments to realizing Noble Purpose. Operating in and through Noble Purpose requires humility and concern for others, that is, servanthood, as seen in Robert Greenleaf's *Servant Leadership*. Greatness is not in more; it is in less. Not less contribution, but less of you as ego and more of you as authentic being, caring and contributing to others.

Claiming is devoid of fear. It is a place of quiet effectiveness, humility, autonomy and fierce resolve. Simultaneously, you surrender to those with whom you work.

Being in the zone of extraordinary Noble Purpose draws people and resources to you. Your attention on Noble Purpose touches the hearts and passions of others galvanizing them into remarkable action. This notion of Claiming comes from a place of inner strength and confidence, that is embedded in your Essential Self. Thus, Claiming combines inner peace and confidence with inspired action and high performance. The resulting inspired performance occurs easily without worry or pain.

In summary, consider the essential parts of Claiming.

Claiming schema:

   1. Be present to your purpose.

2. Establish timing and action plans for the realization of your purpose.

3. Identify material and human resources that you will need.

4. Implement and be responsible for plans and resources needed to accomplish your purpose.

5. Monitor and follow up on service provided.

Claiming in Your Daily Routine

Choose one of the following processes for integrating Claiming into your daily routine. For maximum benefit, it is recommended that you create an affirmation and complete either the anchoring activity, body exercise, ritual, artistic expression, journal writing or aesthetic appreciation, described as follows.

Affirmation

Create an affirmation that emphasizes and/or strengthens a particular implication of this chapter that would assist you in your journey to Noble Purpose. Write the affirmation on an index card or a piece of paper and carry it with you today. Repeat the affirmation several times before lunch, before ending your workday and before retiring in the evening.

For example, "I live my purpose, generating and sustaining service in the world."

Anchoring Activity

Great Claiming exists at the intersection of effective action in the world and deep peace and equanimity. Studies on peak performance demonstrate that high performance occurs when there is perfect stillness, rest, personal ease and intense, focused energy that can move mountains (Csikszentmihalyi 1-8). For most of us, the balance is skewed heavily toward action, for action's sake. This activity focuses on cultivating quiet and silence within.

Create time for solitude and silence that incorporates the following points:

+ Take time to be still. Find alone time. Build it into your schedule.

- Don't misunderstand. This place of silence and perfect equanimity is not designed to displace activity that leads to breakthrough results in the world. It is not a case of either/or but both/and.

- Quiet your mind. Turn off the noise and just be alone, in nature, in an out-of-the-way space at work or at home. Allow yourself to become a receptacle for new information to organize and generate your action. Trust and honor the urges and impulses for Claiming your Noble Purpose.

Body Exercise

Take 10-15 minutes to sit quietly, releasing your thoughts and closing your eyes. Consider the following reflection, focusing on a particular body sensation.

Embodying your purpose requires personal strength, courage and conviction. Such strength, courage and conviction is significantly more generative when grounded in a place of effortless, equanimity and peace. Great Claiming occurs with ease and grace. Scan your body and notice those organs and bodily functions that occur with such ease and grace, day after day, moment after moment. For example, consider your breath, the digestion of your food, the functioning of your heart, etc. Upon choosing an aspect of your body, focus long enough to experience how this aspect of your body is transparent, providing you an essential bodily function without stress, toil or pain. Feel this effortless capacity that so brilliantly serves you. Catch a glimpse of how claiming your Noble Purpose could be similarly transparent and effortless.

Ritual

Become aware of a time in your career when you magnificently fulfilled your purpose, creating brilliantly in the world while simultaneously maintaining effortless, perfect calm. What were you doing? How were you being? How did you feel? Ritually ground that experience in your life by creating a display that depicts that experience and post it on your refrigerator at home or in your work space (e.g., the display could be a picture you draw or the words from a song or a poem that underscores the experience, etc.). What implications does that experience have for your current engagement of your Noble Purpose?

Artistic Expression

Create a Claiming mandala. (Note: a mandala is a visual expression of cherished values and beliefs that indigenous peoples created to symbolize what was important to them). Draw a circle and place an "X" in the middle to create four quadrants. Consider the following four elements that will compose your Claiming mandala:

1. The innate strengths that you claim in order to fulfill your purpose.

2. The resources (human and/or material) you have access to that will be instrumental in fulfilling your purpose.

3. How your purpose will show up in the world, i.e., service.

4. The quality of serenity and/or peace that you claim for yourself in living your Noble Purpose.

Without using words, visualize icons or images that represent each of these dimensions of Claiming and proceed to draw your Claiming mandala with magic markers, colored pencils or chalk.

Journaling Activity

Scan the people that you have worked with over your career and identify the names of one or two who created magnificently in the world while maintaining health and equanimity in the process. Journal about these persons and the inner strengths and resources that they drew upon to achieve such equanimity in their life. Journal about how you might access such inner strength in your life.

Rekindling Awareness for Claiming Through Aesthetic Appreciation

There are many ways to rekindle your awareness for an important idea or thought, changing how you think or feel about some reality in your life/work. Three different forms of aesthetic expression are described below, you may wish to use one or more to rekindle the ideas expressed in this chapter on Claiming. The aesthetic forms include music, poetry and painting. These are only recommendations. You would be well-served to reflect on various forms of aesthetic expression, choosing something you feel drawn to, and then using it to help embed the reality of Claiming in your consciousness.

Music — Find a favorite piece of music that exemplifies Claiming as expressed in the Noble Purpose Spiral and listen to it throughout the day, allowing the lyric or melody to enter your psyche, reinforcing the qualities associated with Claiming. Listen to the music on your drive to work, if feasible at work and/or at home at the end of the day.

Let the River Run by Carly Simon is a song that is infused with the qualities associated with Claiming: "We're coming to the edge; running on the water; coming through the fog; your sons and daughters; let the river run."

Poetry — Of your favorite poems, choose one that contains elements of Claiming in the Noble Purpose Spiral. Record the poem on an index card or a small piece of paper and place it in your pocket. Periodically throughout the day, find the poem and recite it to yourself and to significant others in your life.

"The Journey" is a poem by Mary Oliver that embodies the essential ideas of Claiming. Here is a brief excerpt:

One day you finally knew
what you had to do, and began,
though the voices around you
kept shouting
their bad advice ...

But you didn't stop.
You knew what you had to do

Painting — Consider your favorite paintings and choose a painting that evokes the quality of Claiming for you. Notice how the use of color, texture, shape and form resonate within you and this quality of the Noble Purpose Spiral. Place the painting or a photo or other rendering of the painting in full view so that you can connect with it as you go through the day. If it is inconvenient to take it to work with you, place it in a conspicuous place in your home allowing it to provoke in you the qualities associated with Claiming. If possible to capture the image of this favorite painting electronically, place it as wallpaper in your personal computer so that it greets you throughout the day.

CHAPTER 6

Celebrating

Let the beauty we love be what we do. There are a hundred ways to kneel and kiss the ground.

— Rumi

Really great people have a curious feeling that the greatness is not in them, but through them. And they see something divine in every other person.

— John Ruskin

Celebrating — Experiencing the joy in knowing that your life makes a difference.

The fulfillment of extraordinary Noble Purpose brings great personal satisfaction. Out of this satisfaction you experience unimaginable gratitude for your gifts.

This place of gratitude for the gift of your life is accessible at any time. Living your life from this place of deep appreciation and thanksgiving is part and parcel of having Noble Purpose in the world. It is not dependent on anything other than your waking up and experiencing the goodness of your life and work.

Celebrating encompasses not only the inner experience of rejoicing, feeling gratitude and appreciating, but also the outer, tangible expression of regard, recognition and/or acknowledgment of others.

Inner Dimension of Celebrating

The possibility: You take an appreciative stance, not from a self-serving or egotistic place, but from a place of gratitude for being the unique person you are. Cherishing life as a splendid laboratory for coming to terms with your reason for being serves to realize your Noble Purpose. Experiencing the awe and wonder of life — your relationships, accomplishments and circumstances — sets the field for a deeper and wider fulfillment of your life's purpose.

Kay, a 45-year-old executive director of a non-profit shares this story of how celebrating her story paved the way for a more compassionate response to the troubled youths she served, as well as helping the youths get in touch with their greatness:

When I was two or three years old my parents divorced and my mother was left to raise my three older brothers and me as a single parent. She suffered from manic-depression at a time when effective medication was not yet available.

My childhood experiences of my mother were a series of huge contradictions: from a loving, devoted mother; to a suicidal mother; to a completely crazed mother with outrageous behavior. As a result, during the first 13 years of my life I was moved 26 times, living in orphanages, with foster families, with various relatives and at times with my mother and brothers.

When I was 14 years old, my mother died of cancer and following her death, for the first time, I experienced a long-term stable environment with an aunt. Unfortunately, two of my brothers did not fare as well and lived on their own, sometimes on the streets, from the time they were 14 and 15 years old.

As a very young child, I was familiar with social workers. On several occasions my mother would disappear for long periods of time and neighbors, relatives or teachers would contact the authorities to report her as missing. My brothers would say that the social workers were going to "swoop us up and take us away somewhere."

It is not a big surprise that as an adult I became involved in a helping profession. I had worked for 10 years for the American Red Cross, a wonderful organization. However, I began to feel a strong pull to work with an organization that supported children.

I spent one afternoon visiting a county children's home. Memories of my childhood flooded back, and I became painfully aware of how little of my childhood I had shared with anyone, including my husband and children. As a child, I had always felt the stigma of being different and even as an adult, felt people would never understand my erratic and dysfunctional family pattern and consequently wouldn't understand me.

Synchronously, I received a call from an ex-Red Cross board member who was now serving as a board member for a shelter for runaway and homeless teenagers in the Midwest city where I lived. The executive director position was available and she encouraged me to apply.

I will never forget the evening I interviewed with the six-member search committee. My résumé reflected the person that I presented to the world: competent administrator, college graduate, married, three children and living in an affluent suburb. After several questions, a woman on the search committee who was chairman of the board, asked, "Tell me why someone with your background would be interested in working with troubled youth in the inner-city?"

Well ... I looked at her and I felt my face grow hot and tears started to well-up in my eyes. I fought them back, but it was no use. Tears rolled down my cheeks as I began to tell my childhood stories. Before long others were crying, and we laughed as we passed the tissues amongst us.

I got the position. That was the start of sharing myself with great appreciation for the gifts of empathy, fierce resolve and humility I developed as a result of my childhood. I began to proclaim throughout the community that the children we served were just like all other children — they were only born into different, less-fortunate circumstances.

I learned a powerful lesson. By not being stingy in acknowledging my life and my capacities, I could create the space within the agency for children to tell their stories, honoring their strengths from sometimes splintered and disenfranchised circumstances.

Kay's reflections on her capacity to celebrate are all the more remarkable given that her childhood was fused with significant dissonance. She demonstrates the powerful learning that is possible from such unfortunate family experiences. The revelation provoked by her interview created access to her Essential Self that she would normally not have had. Her life and work became a demonstration of the power of Celebrating.

Celebrating requires consciousness. It requires waking up by creating a different way of holding the circumstances of your life. Telling your story of growing, overcoming challenge and evolving is an important expression of Celebrating.

Cynical and negative stories may need to be rewritten. Repeated telling of your story as one of "gloom and doom" — for example, feeling depleted, insufficient and not able — reinforces these realities in the world, disempowering you and your Noble Purpose. Remember, thought is creative and what you think you generate in the world.

New stories arise out of becoming aware of the diminishment of the current story. The mere release of the old story is also in and of itself an important step forward. And creating a new story can move us into totally new realms of possibility, providing new access to Noble Purpose. Even the most traumatic and oppressive experiences of loss and separation contain the seeds of new learning.

Try it. Celebrate — right now — that aspect of your life that is most challenging, most confronting. Stop. Reflect. Where is the source of your dissonance? Identify the pain and then celebrate the pain. Celebrate that this circumstance is the gateway to a new paradigm from which to create or achieve Noble Purpose. Let go of your predisposition to be victimized by that situation. Look deeply, perhaps for the first time, discovering that this situation is fused with potential for you, that within it is a clue for transforming your current challenge. Consciously give expression to the gifts inherent in your pain and celebrate.

The quality of Celebrating identified here is not some sort of superficial positive thinking. It is totally authentic. It is the grist for the mill necessary to achieve your wildest dreams and ambitions.

Outer Dimension of Celebrating

The rite of passage associated with Initiating lets you know that colleagues you work with are also on their Noble Purpose journey. You see their gifts and talents, even though they may be very different from your own and you realize their potential to powerfully contribute to the work of the team and organization. Celebrating is that quality of the Noble Purpose Spiral that has you give full, unconscious expression of your appreciation of others. This unabashed expression of appreciation represents the important outer dimension of Celebrating.

At the outer level, unconditional regard for colleagues that comes from the heart nurtures those persons. This expression of unconditional regard sows the seeds of Noble Purpose. All that your colleagues want is to be noticed for their contribution. When you authentically celebrate them, you dramatically foster their potential to realize Noble Purpose, shifting the space in which you and they work, provoking remarkable energy and results in the world.

Generous giving of recognition to others is closely coupled to generous receiving of recognition. An important gift you can give others is the welcome embrace of recognition they give to you. Can you recall a time when you felt powerfully acknowledged by someone? Reflect and record your responses in your journal. How did you feel when acknowledged? How did it effect the way you felt about them?

If you resist or deflect the expression of recognition by others, you essentially resist or deflect them. This deflection of others is most likely because you have difficulty celebrating yourself. A sure way to erode Noble Purpose is depreciation and negative self-evaluation.

The ability to celebrate others is inextricably linked with your capacity to celebrate yourself. That is, there is a very intimate linkage between outer and inner dimensions of Celebrating. If you don't celebrate yourself, chances are that it will feel incongruent for you to receive the expression of recognition from another and equally challenging for you to recognize your colleagues.

Powerful Celebrating has you consciously looking for the good in others. It can be subtle — for example, merely considering another person in a positive way, whether expressed or not, changes the ground from which Noble Purpose arises. Expressing your appreciation verbally greatly accelerates the momentum for you and your colleagues in your work together to achieve extraordinary Noble Purpose.

In summary, consider these essential aspects of Celebrating.

Celebrating schema:

1. Be conscious of what you have been doing and who you have been that advances your purpose.

2. Allow yourself to take in and experience gratitude for your gifts and accomplishments.

3. Actively celebrate those accomplishments.

4. Acknowledge what others are doing and who they are.

Applying Celebrating in Your Daily Routine

Choose one of the following processes for integrating Celebrating into your daily routine. For maximum benefit, it is recommended that you create an affirmation and complete either the anchoring activity, body exercise, ritual, artistic expression, journal writing or aesthetic appreciation, described as follows.

Affirmation

Create an affirmation that emphasizes and/or strengthens a particular implication of this chapter that would assist you in your journey to Noble Purpose. Write the affirmation on an index card or a piece of paper and carry it with you. Repeat the affirmation several times before lunch, before ending your workday and before retiring in the evening.

For example, "I experience great gratitude for the bountiful gifts that the universe has bestowed upon me, especially _____ (e.g., family, friends, work, accomplishments, etc.)."

Anchoring Activity

1. Express your appreciation to colleagues at work for how they make a difference for you.

2. Explore Celebrating by expressing your appreciation to three coworkers today by:

    ◆ Recalling concrete details of what they did or said that made a difference for you.

    ◆ Contacting each colleague, scheduling time for visits if necessary.

    ◆ Letting your colleagues know what they did that you valued so highly and why what they did deserves your appreciation.

Body Exercise

Take 10-15 minutes to sit quietly, releasing your thoughts and closing your eyes. Consider the following reflection, focusing on a particular body sensation.

Think of a time when you experienced great appreciation and gratitude for some circumstance in your life, for a valued family member and/or friend or for something that you created or you were gifted with. Notice where in your body you felt this appreciation and gratitude. Focus on that place. Notice your feelings. Be aware of your capacity to return to that place in your body and to that feeling or state throughout your day.

Ritual

Acknowledge yourself today. Reflect on the progress you have made in pursuing your Noble Purpose and treat yourself to a great meal, a special gift or a mini vacation (even a few hours off work) to celebrate your progress and what you have accomplished.

Artistic Expression

Look through old magazines and find four or five images, pictures, advertising messages, etc. that celebrate who you are, in pursuit of your Noble Purpose. Consider those unique qualities as a human being that distinguish you. Cut out these images and create a collage, celebrating yourself as a fully unique expression of a human being.

Journaling Activity

What are your gifts? What is it that you just can't help but provide to those you work with? List three or four of those capacities or traits that colleagues would identify as your gifts. Allow yourself to feel this greatness. What would life and your Noble Purpose look like if you could consistently live out of your gifts? Record your responses in your journal.

Rekindling Awareness for Celebrating Through Aesthetic Expression

There are many ways to rekindle your awareness for an important idea or thought, changing how you think or feel about some reality in your life/work. Three different forms of aesthetic expression are described below, one or more of which you may wish to use to rekindle the ideas expressed in this chapter on Celebrating. The aesthetic forms include music, poetry and painting. These are only recommendations. You would be well served to reflect on various forms of aesthetic expression, choosing something you feel drawn to, and then using it to help embed the reality of Celebrating in your consciousness.

Music — Find a favorite piece of music that exemplifies Celebrating as expressed in the Noble Purpose Spiral and listen to it throughout the day, allowing the lyric or melody to enter your psyche, reinforcing the qualities associated with Celebrating. Listen to the music on your drive to work, if feasible at work and/or at home at the end of the day.

Seasons of Love from the musical *Rent* is infused with the qualities associated with Celebrating:

"Five hundred twenty-five thousand six hundred minutes; 525,600 moments so dear; 525,600 minutes," the lyrics state. "How do you measure — measure a year? In day lights — In sunsets; In midnights — In cups of coffee; In inches — In miles; In laughter — In strife? In 525,600 minutes; How do you measure a year in the life? How about love? How about love? How about love? Measure in love."

Poetry — Of your favorite poems, choose one that contains elements of Celebrating as expressed in the Noble Purpose Spiral. Record the poem on an index card or a small piece of paper and place it in your pocket. Periodically throughout the day, find the poem and recite it to yourself and to significant others in your life.

"Love after Love" is a poem written by Derek Walcott, that embodies the essential ideas of Celebrating. Here is a brief excerpt:

The time will come
when, with elation,
you will greet yourself arriving
at your own door, in your own mirror,
and each will smile at the other's welcome ...

Sit. Feast on your life.

Painting — Consider your favorite paintings and choose a painting that evokes the quality of Celebrating for you. Notice how the use of color, texture, shape and form resonate within you and this quality of the Noble Purpose Spiral. Place the painting or a photo or other rendering of the painting in full view so that you can connect with it as you go through your day. If it is inconvenient to take it to work with you, place it in a conspicuous place in your home allowing it to provoke in you the qualities associated with Celebrating. If possible, capture the image electronically and save it as wallpaper in your personal computer so that it greets you throughout the day.

CHAPTER 7

Letting Go

> *Crisis is always a purification if we understand it correctly. The very word 'crisis' comes from a root that means sifting out. Crisis is a separation, a sifting out of that which is viable and can go on from that which is dead and has to be left behind.*
>
> — *David Steindl-Rast and Sharon Lebell*

Letting Go — Releasing fear and the need for power, control and approval.

Letting Go is the release of fear that prompts desperate clutching, holding on and the use of force and control from two distinct vantage points. First, at an inner level, Letting Go is embracing and releasing the pain associated with a childhood wounding — the Fundamental Dissonance as described in Chapter Two. Second, Letting Go, at an outer level, is entering into and resolving difficult and painful situations with others in life or work, relinquishing the need to safeguard and protect, communicating fully with others.

Inner Level: Letting Go of Force and Control

In early childhood you experienced a Fundamental Dissonance, a traumatic event that prompted you to be fearful, to have self-doubt and, consequently, to withdraw or over compensate in various realms of your life. This wound was often incurred from unintentional and unknowing behaviors of parents, friends or loved ones, or as a result of other life circumstances. This childhood experience prompted ongoing, predictable behavior patterns, continuing through your adult years, even though it may be transparent and not in your consciousness. Other dissonant experiences arising from life/work challenges, throughout your adult years, commingle and become implicated with this originating dissonant childhood episode.

🐿 *Fundamental Dissonance*

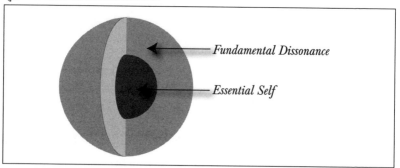

My Fundamental Dissonance was directly related to the frenetic pandemonium and rejection I encountered, on the school bus, during my first days of school. The patterned identity that resulted from my dissonance was "I Don't Fit In." There are many such dissonant childhood identities, such as, "I Am Not A Good Person," "I Don't Matter," "I Am Not Loveable," "I Am Not Enough" and so forth. Notice that closely associated with your dissonant experience is a defining character orientation that influences your behavior and potentially the course of your life.

Jim, a 61-year-old CEO, shares this story of childhood dissonance, prompting him to seize control in his life, ultimately of organizations he would lead. Jim eventually awakens to his persistent need to prevail over all things, achieving significant resolution out of repeated discord and painful encounters.

I grew up in Marin County, California, in a family of five children. Dad was a senior executive for a Fortune 100 company. As a seven-year-old, tragedy struck when my younger brother drowned. Mom fell into a well of grief, struggled with depression and left home for six months of therapy. When Dad, my brother and sisters and I went to pick her up, Mom's first words in an angry voice were, "Why did you bring the kids?" I felt unloved and unwanted. She was really hard on my older brother and me. I mustered all of the control and strength I could summon. I gave sermons in the backyard. I stood on orange crates with a little wooden cross (like the wooden swords we used to carry on our wars and hunts in the lovely nearby hills). I determined that to survive I had to excel, to be larger than life. I played three sports, was class valedictorian and made it into Princeton. At the Harvard Business School, friends would call me the Prussian General because of my certainty and invincibility.

After Harvard, at age 28, I joined the company where my father was now CEO. I moved up through the ranks, becoming president of a $50 million division, which was spun off. As part of the company's sale, I was made CEO and part owner. I was on my way to fame and fortune.

I then entered the Time of Troubles: between the age of 42 and 46. At 42, my wife died of cancer. My company went broke. I helped acquire another company that went bankrupt. I lost most of what I had, but I felt invincible enough to acquire another company that was hugely profitable, with a purchase price of $35 million. I put up $200,000 and others provided the rest. I owned 46 percent of the voting stock. Four months later, I was fired. The former owner didn't like what I was doing with his business; he particularly objected to my seeing his daughter who worked at the company.

I retreated to my backyard garden, where I felt the pain of my life, the bungling of business deals and the loss of loved ones. My drive to be extraordinary and the hero did not succeed in relationships, in business or in the world. I knew I could no longer sustain being first and all-conquering. I fully let in the pain and pondered the deeper implications of being human. I could no longer sustain the burden of being first, responsible for everything. What emerged in me was a strange kind of peace and grace and respect for the goodness of life.

At 46, after much time sitting, reading and reflecting, after fully experiencing the reverses in my personal and business life, I was invited back out into the world. One morning I went fishing with a friend who was chairman of the board of a major Southeastern city aquarium project, a fledgling adventure, with a big dream and no money. He invited me to take it on. I was "hooked," and an amazing odyssey, that played a large role in my spiritual awakening, was about to begin.

The aquarium was my first experience of leading without power. There was no cash in the bank. I had no political clout in this city. I didn't know anything about architecture, bonds or fish. So where does one go? I went within, to the deep trust that had begun to come to light, and I went to the dream. I invited others to bring their gifts and their passions. The team formed around our collective dream, drawn to the circle that would create this project.

The Prussian General was still there, but he had grown a bit wiser, a little humbler. There were some decisions I had to make. Not many, but some. Often I wouldn't have a clue and would tell the team I was taking two days off to meditate in my garden. They respected this. There was an amazing combination of deep listening to each other and fierce accountability. We are taught that this soft and fuzzy stuff doesn't lead to hard-nosed, bottom-line success, but I disagree. I have never seen a team that held each other more accountable, but yet listened, in fact, truly loved each other. Over and over again, the miracles would happen, the people or resources would show up just when they were needed. We lost our site, our equity, our bank and our political support at least once in each case ... but this team would not be denied.

The aquarium, ultimately a $100 million project, is now a centerpiece of this major Southeastern city's downtown development and a great community resource. With the construction of the aquarium, I began to build confidence in my newfound self. I remember, then I forget. I let go of my pain, fear, my need to be invincible and live, for a time, in the fullest expression of my inner capacities, inviting others into this same

space. There is no greater calling and no greater joy than to share the
power of remembering our wholeness, connecting the mind, the heart
and the soul.

Two Manifestations of Fundamental Dissonance

There are two eventualities arising from your Fundamental Dissonance. Like most of us, Jim the CEO illustrates aspects of both, but particularly of the second manifestation. First, you end up resisting and thus becoming the dissonance, mimicking the old adage, "what you resist, you become." As a result, you are possessed by the experience, immobilized and disempowered and, consequently, you avoid situations or circumstances that remotely resemble the initial wounding experience.

The second and more common likelihood is tenaciously working to go beyond your Fundamental Dissonance, very much as Jim illustrates. You become a Superman or Superwoman, "leaping tall buildings in a single bound." The "building" being your childhood dissonance. The resulting heroics to get beyond your pain is personified in the Bounded Self. For example, feeling not smart enough as a child (dissonant experience) could foster needing to "know it all" throughout your adult life. Or, feeling not good enough as a child could prompt a Herculean need to get to the top. While being tenacious is a testament to your capacity to get beyond your dissonance, it is often depleting and further separating you from your fundamental goodness and the strength of your Essential Self.

The outward manifestation of your Bounded Self belies the compassion and sensitivity of your Essential Self. You rely on force, control and manipulation — to do whatever it takes — to either leap beyond or avoid the circumstances of your dissonance. The Enron debacle, as well as a plethora of other socially irresponsible business practices, likely emanated from leaders who were compelled to wield excessive power as the aftermath of persisting dissonant experiences.

Given that childhood wounding is part and parcel of being a human being, what is there to do? As suggested earlier, life has a way of providing "jolts," in the form of challenging life transitions, which create cracks in the hard, impermeable veneer of the Bounded Self. The cracks catapult you through your dissonance and to the magic of your unbounded, Essential Self.

There is another alternative to this cracking open. It is Letting Go, becoming conscious of and embracing your Fundamental Dissonance. As long as you resist, attempting to escape or to go beyond your dissonance, the childhood emotional trauma remains logged within you. You attempt to escape. There is no escaping. Pain of the present merges with the pain of the past, and the dissonance continues largely as a result of the unconscious resistance to the pain.

Letting Go in the midst of this is surrendering into the painful thoughts and feelings. It is fully allowing and feeling your thoughts and feelings. Observe and discern them. Give them space. Notice what particular sensations occur in your body. Record your feelings in your journal or notebook as you notice them. When you accept your dissonance fully, you are no longer compelled to act out your resistance. Out of embracing and entering into the Fundamental Dissonance, it dissipates. Thus with Letting Go comes a new freedom and the liberation from behaviors that undergird the Bounded Self.

Letting Go Visualization

Before you can embrace you must become conscious of your Fundamental Dissonance, giving this identity a name. Use the following, simple visualization and writing exercise to assist you in identifying your Fundamental Dissonance. As you begin to review this exercise, know that it is not unusual to feel lethargic, resistant or unwilling to proceed. Persist. Penetrate through your resistance as great benefit can result from this exercise. If you feel you have not gotten to your core dissonance through the exercise, you may want to seek professional help from a counselor, therapist or trusted friend to assist you in reflecting on and identifying your most dissonant childhood experience.

1. Find a secluded, comfortable, quiet place, where you can enter into this visualization and journal. You may wish to play suitable, calming and soothing music that creates a contemplative mood for your reflection and writing.

2. Close your eyes and fully relax. Take a deep breath. At this time, there is nothing to organize, nothing to grasp, nothing to do. Simply follow your breath.

3. Return yourself to early positive childhood memories, going as far back as you can, to age three, four, five, six or seven. Focus on a positive experience that comes to mind. Notice where you are, who is present and the circumstances. Notice how you feel. Let it all in, feeling the satisfaction of the moment. Be aware of what you experience. Savor the experience.

4. When you are ready, allowing sufficient time to fully experience your feelings, turn to your journal or notepad and record these positive experiences in detail.

5. Once complete, return to your quiet, contemplative state and close your eyes. Receive into your attention any unpleasant, unsettling experiences from childhood. Recall difficult and challenging communications with friends and others; with your parents or family; with some negative, extenuating circumstances. Allow an image to announce itself which graphically captures the torment or confrontational nature of a highly disappointing, frightening, defaming or degrading experience. Note what particular sensations occur in your body. Scan other challenging experiences to determine if this is your Fundamental Dissonance.

6. When you have arrived at your Fundamental Dissonance and you are fully present to your experience, turn to your journal or notepad and record these unpleasant experiences and the related feelings. Write in detail about your experience.

7. When complete, name the negative identity that you assigned to yourself in the course of that traumatic experience. Continue to journal about the facts related to the situation and, most importantly, about your emotional response and sensations in your body, fully allowing yourself to feel.

8. When you have deeply felt everything about this challenging childhood circumstance and the feelings have begun to dissipate, bring closure to

your writing. In completing your reflection, notice what occurs to you when you don't resist these negative feelings. How would you characterize your state now? What are the implications of allowing for and embracing your Fundamental Dissonance?

Successful Letting Go fully embraces your Fundamental Dissonance. As long as you resist, attempting to escape or to go beyond your dissonance, your childhood dissonance persists. Dissonance continues largely as a result of the unconscious resistance to your pain. The opposite of resisting is to surrender into the pain, fully feeling your dissonant emotions and thoughts, observing and discerning them. When you accept your Dissonant Self, fully, you are no longer a captive of your dissonance.

Outer Level: Letting Go To Resolve Difficult or Painful Situations with Others

There is a second and important outer notion of Letting Go, which results from dissonant relationships with others. Honest differences of opinion or divergent temperaments and personality orientations can foster interpersonal tensions among coworkers, friends and family. Such tensions inhibit open communications and displace the honoring and regard of others that is ascribed in Initiating and acclaimed in Celebrating. Consequently, you may withhold communications, inauthentically relating to others, safeguarding yourself from entering into a potentially unpleasant communication. Letting Go invites you to enter into such communications, providing authentic, straight, clear, forthright communications that are absolutely respectful of others, releasing all force, control and manipulation. Such personal integrity and capacity to communicate how you think and feel, pierces through your self-consciousness, promoting healing for you and others.

Entering into such difficult interpersonal matters will likely require one of two broad forms of communication. In the first form of communication, you disclose thoughts and feelings about yourself that you may feel somewhat uncomfortable sharing. In the second form, you share thoughts and feelings about others, providing constructive feedback.

Living your Noble Purpose requires boldness and courage in sharing how you think and feel. It also requires you to be impeccable in how you communicate your thinking, feelings and respect for others. (See Appendix B for a simple, yet powerful process for expressing yourself and your pain, with friends or colleagues when a breakdown occurs.)

Karlfried Gras von Durkheim encourages fully entering into that which is dissonant in you, others or life as a path to greater wholeness. Durkheim also points to the kind of support required from others to remain true to your path:

Only to the extent that man exposes himself over and over again to annihilation, can that which is indestructible arise within him. In this lies the dignity of daring. Thus, the aim of practice is not to develop an attitude which allows a man to acquire a state of harmony and peace wherein nothing can ever trouble him.

On the contrary, practice ... should enable him to dare to let go of his futile hankering after harmony, surcease from pain, and a comfortable life in order that he may discover, in doing battle with the forces that oppose him, that which awaits him beyond the world of opposites. The first necessity is that we should have the courage to face life, and to encounter all that is most perilous in the world ...

The more a man learns wholeheartedly to confront the world that threatens him with isolation, the more are the depths of the ground of being revealed in the possibilities of new life and becoming opened.

As Durkheim implies, go into the pain, feel the pain, "becoming opened, encountering all that is most perilous in the world ... exposing one's self over and over again to annihilation, allowing that which is indestructible within" to arise. The perfection of life is not separate from the pain; it exists in and through the pain.

A life of Noble Purpose that calls you to go beyond your self-imposed limitations, to take risks, may provoke disappointments, breakdowns and pain that flares up your Fundamental Dissonance.

In this instance, Letting Go clears the air between individuals, allowing for the completion of unexpressed issues and concerns that have been preoccupations. An important outcome of great Letting Go is a new freedom to communicate with others in responsible ways that respect the dignity of those individuals while being fully authentic.

In summary, consider these essential parts of Letting Go.

Letting Go schema:

1. Identify and embrace your Fundamental Dissonance from childhood, allowing yourself to completely feel these feelings.

2. Notice when you don't engage in your life due to fear of failure or not being approved by others and feel those feelings and thoughts without resistance.

3. Notice when you use power and control, manipulating your environment or others to achieve those results, and become aware of the underlying fear that provokes those tendencies and fully feel that fear, and those feelings and thoughts, without resistance.

4. Communicate forthrightly with others, disclosing your feelings, providing constructive feedback.

Letting Go in Your Daily Routine

Choose one of the following processes for integrating Letting Go into your daily routine. For maximum benefit, it is recommended that you create an affirmation and complete either the anchoring activity, body exercise, ritual, artistic expression, journal writing or aesthetic appreciation, described as follows.

Affirmation

Create an affirmation that emphasizes and/or strengthens a particular implication of this chapter that would assist you in your journey to extraordinary Noble Purpose. Write the affirmation on an index card or a piece of paper and carry it with you today. Repeat the affirmation several times before lunch, before ending your work day and before retiring in the evening.

For example, "I let go of all fear, anxiety, worry or concern about my Noble Purpose, knowing that the fruits of my labor can powerfully affect change in the world."

Anchoring Activity

How do you tap into the expansive sense of freedom, associated with the Essential Self that Letting Go can make possible? Stop holding-on. Relinquish your tenacious grasping to realize or discover your Noble Purpose for one whole day. Stop the relentless clutching or need to fulfill your Noble Purpose. Let go, noticing all of the incredible gifts in your life, irrespective of your Noble Purpose ever being discovered or realized. Know that such neediness diminishes your capacity to discern or realize Noble Purpose. Suspending your need to accomplish allows access to your inner-most wisdom and, paradoxically, to new glimpses of Noble Purpose.

Body Exercise

Sit quietly for 10-15 minutes, releasing your thoughts and closing your eyes. Consider the following reflection, focusing on a particular body sensation.

Be aware of tightness, strain or anxiety in your body. Go deeply into that place and embrace it fully. Allow the strain or anxiety to greatly magnify, feel it grow within you and then hold that place for 30 seconds. During the 30 seconds notice its shape, its color, its weight, mass and dimension. Experience it fully, then release that place. Repeat this practice a second time.

Ritual

Record on a piece of paper any sources of unease or dissonance that you are experiencing regarding your Noble Purpose. Leave sufficient space between each source of frustration or worry, so that when finished recording you can tear the paper apart, leaving frustration on a separate piece of paper. In a fireplace or a simple urn (even an ash tray) ritually burn each piece of paper. As you light each paper identifying a frustration, allow yourself to release any tension or worry that you feel and proceed to do this for all of your frustrations.

Artistic Expression

Buy a few cans of modeling clay. Begin this activity by getting in touch with the greatest source of dissonance that you are experiencing regarding the fulfillment of your Noble Purpose while shaping the clay in your hands. As you experience the dissonance allow your hands to mold the clay into any image that comes to mind. Allow yourself to spontaneously form the clay. Take your time. When complete, pick up a second piece of clay and then consider what it would be like if you were to have a breakthrough regarding this situation. Allow yourself to feel the sense of freedom at having such a breakthrough and, as you do that, fashion the second piece of clay into an object. As before, let it happen spontaneously. When finished, place the two pieces that you sculpted side-by-side and reflect on the insights you have gleaned.

Journaling Activity

Create three columns on one of your journal pages and label them as follows:

1. Disappointment/frustration.

2. Opportunity.

3. Action.

Notice the greatest obstacles or frustrations that are confronting you in achieving extraordinary Noble Purpose. Allow yourself to feel at your depths, the disappointment, worry, concern or anger that you feel about this obstacle. Journal and record those feelings noting their relationship to your Fundamental Dissonance. Experience these fully. In the second column, begin to reflect on how this obstacle has been an opportunity. How has it caused you to grow, to be more creative, more resilient? In the third column, consider and write about actions that are calling you forth right now. Distinguish between two kinds of actions — those that diminish the frustration or disappointment and those that enhance the opportunity currently presenting itself.

Rekindling Awareness for Letting Go Through Aesthetic Appreciation

There are many ways to rekindle your awareness for an important idea or thought, changing how you think or feel about some reality in your life/work.

Three different forms of aesthetic expression are described below, one or more of which you may wish to use to rekindle the ideas expressed in this chapter on Letting Go. The aesthetic forms include music, poetry and painting. These are only recommendations. You would be well served to reflect on various forms of aesthetic expression, choosing something you feel drawn to, and then using it to help embed the reality of Letting Go in your consciousness.

Music — Find a favorite piece of music that exemplifies Letting Go as expressed in the Noble Purpose Spiral and listen to it throughout the day, allowing the lyric or melody to enter your psyche, reinforcing the qualities associated with Letting Go. Listen to the music on your drive to work, if feasible at work and/or at home at the end of the day.

Bridge Over Troubled Water is a song that is infused with the qualities associated with Letting Go:

"When you're weary; Feeling small; When tears are in your eyes; I will dry them all; I'm on your side; Oh, when times get rough; And friends just can't be found; Like a bridge; Over troubled water; I will lay me down."

Poetry — Of your favorite poems, choose one that contains elements of Letting Go as expressed in the Noble Purpose Spiral. Record the poem on an index card or a small piece of paper and place it in your pocket. Periodically throughout the day, find the poem and recite it to yourself and to significant others in your life.

The poem "Lost," by David Wagoner, embodies the essential ideas of Letting Go. Here is a brief excerpt:

Stand still. The trees ahead and bushes beside you
Are not lost. Wherever you are is called Here ...

The forest knows
Where you are. You must let it find you.

Painting — Consider your favorite paintings and choose a painting that evokes the quality of Letting Go for you. Notice how the use of color, texture, shape and form resonate within you and this quality of the Noble Purpose

Spiral. Place the painting or a photo or other rendering of the painting in full view so that you can connect with it as you go through the day. If it is inconvenient to take it to work with you, place it in a conspicuous place in your home allowing it to provoke in you the qualities associated with Letting Go. If it is possible to capture the image of this favorite painting electronically, save it as wallpaper on your personal computer so that it greets you throughout the day.

CHAPTER 8

Noble Purpose

This is the true joy in life, the being used for a purpose recognized by yourself as a mighty one; the being a force of nature instead of a feverish, selfish little clod of ailments and grievances, complaining that the world will not devote itself to making you happy ... I am of the opinion that my life belongs to the whole community and as long as I live it is my privilege to do for it whatever I can.

I want to be thoroughly used up when I die, for the harder I work, the more I live. I rejoice in life for its own sake. Life is no 'brief candle' to me. It is a sort of splendid torch which I have got hold of for the moment, and I want to make it burn as brightly as possible before handing it on to future generations.

— George Bernard Shaw

Noble Purpose — Realizing your calling and potential by embracing the qualities of the Noble Purpose Spiral.

Note that this chapter contains a particularly lengthy process that requires up to three hours of reflection and journaling. It is recommended that the process be completed in three separate sessions lasting about an hour each. Please plan your time accordingly.

Your Essential Self seeks to manifest its unique, signature form of Noble Purpose resulting in contribution and service to others, regardless of the scope or scale of that contribution. It is fundamental to who you are, your reason for being, involving intellect, heart and spirit. Your Essential Self is understood through the qualities of the Noble Purpose Spiral, and it is through these qualities that you realize your Noble Purpose in the world.

Zone of Noble Purpose

From the research on optimal work performance (Csikszentmihalyi 1-8), we know that when you fully express your unique capacities, time disappears. There is a perfect harmony, a fusion of craft and person. Ego vanishes and what remains is unadulterated service to humanity.

In this space of flow you receive the gift of synchronicity — that is, unexpected and insightful occurrences that forward your purpose in the world. Unexpected awakenings during your sleep reveal exactly the information you need to take that critical next step. Walking in nature or being in silence generates an important shift in your frame of mind — how you think, feel, relate to and ultimately realize your purpose. You become a great artist in your life.

In 1923, Robert Henri said, "When the artist is alive in any person, whatever his kind of work may be, he becomes an inventive, searching, daring, self-expressing creature. He becomes interesting to other people. He disturbs, upsets, enlightens and he opens ways for a better understanding … He does not have to be a painter or sculptor to be an artist. He can work in any medium. He simply has to find the gain in the work itself, not outside of it" (*The Art Spirit* 15).

The Inner Level

In addition to serving others, Noble Purpose is serving yourself, providing what you need/want in life. Your physical health and well-being are correlated with your capacity to access and live your purpose. Lots of people these days report burn-out and exhaustion. The remedy for exhaustion is not rest — it is personal renewal which entails being fully alive and passionate and being in touch with your Noble Purpose. Being in nature, journaling or meditating returns you to personal tranquility and are examples of this renewal. Being able to just be, to listen and respond compassionately to your needs and to discover new resourcefulness in your life are necessary to living Noble Purpose.

Sometimes you may feel adrift or removed from your Noble Purpose. This is not only to be expected, it can be beneficial to you in the long run, much like the re-awakening that occurs in the process of rice paddy cultivation in the East.

Rice paddy seedlings are literally uprooted from the safe, secure waterbeds where they lay fallow and placed on arid soil for two or three days to dry. The rice paddy seedlings experience a threat to their existence as they are forced to cling to life in the hot sun. Later, when replanted, the seedlings powerfully generate roots into the soil. This process yields eight to 10 times as much rice than allowing the plants to grow undisturbed.

The message: Create space for your feelings of being disconnected or uprooted. The challenge is not to invalidate yourself, others or your Noble Purpose. Know that this arid space is far more mysterious and nurturing than you may immediately appreciate. Even the resulting discomfort and dissonance is generative. Respect it. Give yourself a break. Relax. Noble Purpose requires the full spectrum of human experience, including the feeling of being removed from your Noble Purpose. With attention and intention, extraordinary Noble Purpose will emerge at the appointed time.

Death, the Essential Self and Noble Purpose

A dream, involving many of the threads interwoven in this book, shook me to my roots. I awoke in a cold sweat, short of breath, feeling a deep sense of gratitude for life.

A great eye-opening view of my life and the life of the planet was prominent in the dream. Unexplainable shifts in the infrastructure and chemical balance of the planet created a cataclysmic tragedy. The earth was erupting, heaving and undulating. Calamity reined everywhere. All of the peoples of the world, both in developed and emerging economies, were gripped in fear.

At the onset of the tragedy, I was facilitating a class session with students at a university in the Midwest. What was happening and why it was happening was inexplicable. The university building I occupied began to shake and shudder. Plaster fell from the ceiling. A nearby building was ablaze. High winds catapulted trees, cars and parts of buildings through the air. The plumbing exploded in our building and water began to rise. As the water rose, we scampered to higher elevations. Before long the wind jostled the building, and, as the building was lifted into the air, water gushed out to the surging earth below.

The students and I clutched desperately as the building was hurled through the air. We peered out the window in our lecture hall, like a cockpit of a spacecraft hurtling through infinity. Buildings, trees, homes and automobiles were flying through the air in every direction and we were terrified.

Throughout the dream, a Steven Walters tune called *Nothing Less Than Everything* echoed through my psyche. I was comforted by this music. The lyrics treated the existential ache of all humanity:

> *Then I got down on my knees*
> *And begged for mercy*
> *And I raised up my hands*
> *And I knew the answer*
> *Even as I asked the question of*
> *Just how much this love demands*
>
> *And it's everything, everything*
> *Nothing less than everything will do*
> *And when everything is burned*
> *I will take these ashes and*
> *Offer them up to you*

And then imminent disaster confronted us as we were heading directly toward a huge stationary building directly in front of us. Unexpectedly, my fear subsided. I experienced a deep peace and sincere gratitude for the incredible bounty of my life. For seconds, maybe a minute, I dwelled in this ecstasy. At the very last moment the wind buffeting our building shifted, and we missed the huge structure.

I awakened feeling both exhausted and overwhelmed. But superceding all of this was a sense of transcendence, as I was able to see and appreciate the perfection of the universe at the very moment when my death seemed certain. In that moment I descended fully to my Essential Self. Overriding everything was a realization that death was trivial in the face of such extraordinary grace that subsumes all of life and death.

In that same moment, my Noble Purpose infused every cell in my body. I was fully aware of my purpose to foster deep belonging, unbridled freedom and service in the workplace.

The encounter with death was necessary to the dream. The Bounded Self by definition has a preoccupation with death — a great fear. This notion of death is intimately related to our worst fear — the demise of our ideas, projects, commitments, relationships and ultimately the end of our lives.

Thomas Merton observes, "If we become obsessed with the idea of death hiding and waiting for us in ambush … life is divided against itself. Death then operates in the midst of life, not the end of life but, rather, as the fear of life. Death is life afraid to love and trust itself because it is obsessed with its … own ending."

The choice is quite simply life or death. You can choose the love, trust and belonging of Initiating or the fear, resignation and self-doubt that creeps into the cracks and crevices of the larger society and imbues you as an individual.

Noble Purpose Culminating Process

In this process, you are invited to consider your Noble Purpose through the lens of your Essential Self that transcends ordinary life and death. You will bring your purpose, already encoded within you, powerfully into the world as a concise statement. With respect to the mechanics, you will prepare a short statement affirming your Noble Purpose and contribution. It should go beyond your immediate job or role in the world, and begin with, "My purpose is …"

Your statement of Noble Purpose, supported by numerous other elements in this process, will serve as a moment-by-moment reminder of who you are in the world. In the first of the three segments of this process, you will learn how to create your statement of purpose.

In the following three-part process you will alternate between reflection journaling, dialogue exercises in your journal and capturing material from your journal, recording it on index cards. Consider the following icons for each of these three components:

1. Dialogue   2. Reflection   3. Index Card

These icons will be used to alert you to the composition of the various parts of the processes to follow.

In order to complete this process you will need a journal or notepad to respond to the questions and a dozen index cards, that will contain important aspects of your Noble Purpose. The process begins first with consideration of your Noble Purpose globally based on those people whom you most admire in the world, then narrowing to your Noble Purpose as it relates to customers, clients or colleagues served by your contribution. Finally you will create catalytic being and action guidelines for realizing your purpose. This visualization and writing exercise will assist you in getting in touch with your Noble Purpose in each of these separate ways. Be aware that this chapter is not a quick read. You are invited to take an hour or so for each of the three segments of this process, perhaps spreading your work out over a full day.

Segment A: Noble Purpose Figures

Find a secluded, comfortable, quiet place where you can enter into this visualization and journal. You may wish to play suitable, calming music that creates a contemplative mood for your reflection and writing.

Close your eyes and fully relax. Take a deep breath. At this time, there is nothing to organize, nothing to grasp, nothing to do. Simply follow your breath and allow it to carry you into the next moment. Be aware of the chair you are seated on and how it supports you. Slowly scan your body from the top of your head to the bottom of your feet. Be aware of any tension you feel in your body and release it.

1. Noble Purpose Figures

Draw two vertical lines in your journal or notepad, creating three separate columns. Title the first column "Noble Purpose Figure." Reflect on those people in life whom you highly regard — people you are in awe of and greatly respect because of their contribution and what you have learned from them. They can be family members, friends, teachers, heroes, mythical figures or famous people. Create a list of Noble Purpose figures in the first column. When finished, close your eyes and fully relax. Take a deep breath.

Title the second column, "Noble Purpose Contribution." Record in two or three words the contribution that you associate with each Noble Purpose figure — e.g., for your Aunt Helen, "fun-loving and generous." (Important: Look beyond the role these figures play in the world to their essence as human beings. Therein lies their Noble Purpose.) As you add to the second column, feel free to add more people in the first column. When complete, be aware of any tension you feel in your body and release it.

Title the third column, "Learning." What did you learn from your Noble Purpose figures? Record your response in the third column. It is possible the most compelling lessons learned from some of the people on your list was their contribution. For others, the two may be very different — i.e., their contribution may be "fun-loving" while what you learned may be "being authentic" and so forth. As you add to the third column, feel free to add material to the other columns at any time. Take time to savor the list and what these people brought to the world. On a blank page of your journal or notepad, record anything you are feeling or thinking about your list of Noble Purpose figures, their contributions and/or what you learned. When finished, close your eyes and fully relax. Take a deep breath. Be still.

2. Noble Purpose Contemplation

Choose the Noble Purpose figure whose purpose and contribution stands out most for you. On a new page of your journal or notepad, record a reflection about this person drawing upon the qualities of the Noble Purpose Spiral. Specifically, name what stood out most for you about this person's:

1. Trust in the goodness of life and sense of belonging (Initiating).

2. Ability to reveal new possibilities (Visioning).

3. Commitment to realizing results, being his/her Noble Purpose (Claiming).

4. Capacity to fully celebrate life/work (Celebrating).

5. Ability to release power and control (Letting Go).

Add anything else that comes to mind regarding your Noble Purpose figure — whether related or not to the Spiral. Now, take a leap and consider that your Noble Purpose figure is you. That the characteristics you identified for this person you have such great affinity for, reflect your essential fervor, zeal and relationship to the world. Yes, the Noble Purpose figure you specified demonstrates these characteristics, but take a breath and allow yourself to understand that to a very significant extent you embody these attributes. Reread your journal. Allow yourself to embrace the realization that you embody the contributions of all of your Noble Purpose figures. Return to your journal or notepad and record feelings, sensations and realizations as a result of accepting these aspects of your Noble Purpose figures as your own. When finished, relax before moving on to the next part of this process.

3. Noble Purpose Attributes

Create a heading in the center of one of your index cards, "Noble Purpose Cards," followed by today's date, using this card as the cover for a series of cards that you will compile as a part of this process. At the top of a second card create the title, "Noble Purpose Attributes." Below it list the characteristics you noted for your selected Noble Purpose figure, as well as the characteristics of other Noble Purpose figures on your list to which you are especially drawn. Once again, relax, close your eyes for a few seconds and savor these qualities as reflections of your Essential Self.

4. Noble Purpose Statement

Reflect on the characteristics noted on your "Noble Purpose Attributes" card. Return to the process in Chapter Four on pages 40-43, noticing your journal entries regarding the sources of energy in your life/work. Take time to scan now any other relevant previously completed journal entries that provide you further insight about your Noble Purpose and then follow these steps:

- Express your Noble Purpose in a few words; as an affirmative statement about your intended contribution using an action verb.

- Try to expand your statement beyond your immediate job or role in the world.

- Begin with a purpose. "My purpose is…
    … fostering health and vitality for those I serve."
    … generating breakthrough technologies in the financial industry."
    … being fully compassionate and providing encouragement for young children."
    … explosively creating my chosen art form."
    In my case, the statement is as follows: "My purpose is to foster deep belonging, unbridled freedom and service in the workplace."

Begin by recording a working statement of your Noble Purpose in your journal or notepad and then, over the course of the next few days, return to your statement and see if it still powerfully calls to you. Modify and finalize it as you complete the other parts of this process.

Title one of your Noble Purpose cards "Noble Purpose Statement," followed by your purpose statement. Once again, relax, close your eyes for a few seconds and savor this statement of your Noble Purpose. Know that you can return to this card at any time to get in touch with your Noble Purpose and/or to revise or reframe it to more closely fit your purpose in the world. Take a minute or so and relax.

5. Noble Purpose Dialogue

Reflect on the various qualities of the Noble Purpose Spiral, choosing one that you suspect most impinges on the accomplishment of your Noble

Purpose (i.e., a quality that, if not fully realized, could diminish the accomplishment of your Noble Purpose). The spiral represents the critical process considerations that surround the content of your life. A core element of the content of your life is Noble Purpose.

On a new page of your journal or notepad, draw a vertical line down the center of the page. Record the Noble Purpose figure you chose previously at the top of the first column. Write your name, or simply "Me," at the top of the second column. When ready, engage in a dialogue with your Noble Purpose figure about your Noble Purpose and the quality of the spiral that is most crucial to the realization of your Noble Purpose.

Pose a question. Record your question in writing under the second column — e.g., "How best can I embrace and bring this quality of the spiral into my life and work?" Allow time for thoughts to emerge and then record your Noble Purpose figure's response. Really listen. Listen from your Essential Self. Change columns and record your response to the Noble Purpose figure's ideas/thinking.

Alternate back and forth, allowing your thoughts and the thoughts of your Noble Purpose figure to freely express themselves. Don't become too analytical. Just let the exercise happen and receive the special messages that it provides. Before completing your dialogue ask your wisdom figure, "What do you percieve as my greatest strength among the qualitites of the Noble Purpose Spiral?" When finished, close your eyes and fully relax. Take a deep breath.

What occurred for you out of this dialogue process? Record your responses in your journal or notepad. What do you notice now about your Noble Purpose? What quality of the spiral do you need to embrace? What are you being called to do to create momentum in realizing your Noble Purpose? Record your responses in your journal or notepad. When finished, close your eyes and take a deep breath.

6. Noble Purpose Spiral Quality

Title one of your Noble Purpose cards "Quality of (name a quality here) in the Noble Purpose Spiral." On the card, record your most energetic thoughts, ideas and/or actions. Finally, relax and close your eyes. Take a deep breath. Follow your breath and allow it to carry you into the next moment. Scan your body from the top of your head, slowly, to the bottom of your feet. Be aware of any tension you feel and release it.

Note: You may wish to rest or remove yourself from this exploration, continuing on to Segment B of this process some other time. Organize your time, space, life and work so that you can go to the next segment fully energized. Gather together the three Noble Purpose cards that you completed: "Noble Purpose Attributes," "Noble Purpose Statement" and "Quality of _____ in the Noble Purpose Spiral" — you will return to these in Segments B and C of this process.

Segment B: Noble Purpose Beneficiaries

As before, find a comfortable, quiet place away from others where you can visualize and journal. You may wish to play soothing music to create an appropriate mood for your reflection and writing.

Close your eyes and fully relax. Take a deep breath. At this time there is nothing to organize, nothing to grasp, nothing to do. Follow your breath and allow it to carry you into the next moment. Be aware of the chair you are seated on and how it supports you. Scan your body from the top of your head to the bottom of your feet. Notice any tension you feel. Release it.

1. Noble Purpose Beneficiary List

In your journal or notepad, draw a single vertical line down the middle of the page, creating two separate columns. Title the first column "Noble Purpose Beneficiaries." Reflect on those persons in your life who currently benefit from your Noble Purpose or, alternatively, if you are recreating your Noble Purpose, identify those persons who you would most like to serve and benefit from your gifts and talents. Don't compromise yourself. List people who are ideal for receiving your contribution and to whom you are instinctively drawn. They may be people whom you are currently serving or whom you served in the past. They can also be family members, friends, colleagues or others served as a result of your Noble Purpose. When finished compiling your list, close your eyes and fully relax. Allow yourself to experience the remarkable array of people, both those in your life who are touched by you and you by them. Take a deep breath. Relax and be still.

Title the second column "Qualities of My Beneficiaries." Record a few words about the uniqueness of each beneficiary identified in column one, noting especially what you most appreciate about that person. For example, you might appreciate a beneficiary because he/she purchases your services or products, because he/she is a big supporter of your gifts and talents or because you simply enjoy his/her company. As you add to this column, feel free to go back to the first column and include additional beneficiaries. When complete, stop and relax. If you like, close your eyes. Become conscious of the incredible gifts that your beneficiaries bring to you and the affinity you feel for them. Savor these feelings.

2. Noble Purpose Contemplation

Choose the beneficiary to whom you feel most drawn, one who is a great supporter of yours and the gifts you bring to the world. On a new page of your journal or notepad, record a reflection about this person, concretely identifying those personal and other qualities that you most appreciate about him or her. Much like your Noble Purpose figure, consider that this person is you, reflecting your special uniqueness, talent, forte and genius in the world. Allow yourself to take in — fully — that to a very significant extent you embody these qualities. Return to your journal or notepad and record feelings, sensations and realizations as a result of accepting these aspects of your beneficiary as your own. When finished, scan all of the qualities of the beneficiaries of your first list, recording in your journal those that especially resonate within you. Now, fully relax. If you like, close your eyes. Take a deep breath.

3. Noble Purpose Attributes

Title a new Noble Purpose card, "Noble Purpose Attributes," like the one you created in the first segment. On this index card, record all of those unique qualities that you identified in your journal for your beneficiary and other beneficiaries that you feel most drawn to in your life and work. Savor these qualities, realizing that they are an expression of your Essential Self. Take a minute or so to relax.

4. Noble Purpose Dialogue

On a new page of your journal or notepad, draw a vertical line down the center of the page. Record your beneficiary at the top of the first column. Place your name or "Me" at the top of the second column. When ready, engage in a dialogue with your beneficiary about your statement of Noble Purpose as well as a quality of the Spiral that might be implicated in your achieving your extraordinary Noble Purpose. Pose a question. For example, "What might I do to truly realize and be my Noble Purpose in the world?" Record your question under the second column. Allow a moment for the thought or response to emerge and then record the beneficiary's response. Really discern and listen for the response. Change columns and record your beneficiary's response to your question. Alternate back and forth, allowing your thoughts and the thoughts of your beneficiary to freely express themselves. As in the first segment of this process, don't get too analytical — let the exercise happen and receive the special messages that it provides. When finished, close your eyes. Take a deep breath. Notice your breath.

What occurred for you in this process? Record your responses in your journal or notepad. What do you notice now about your Noble Purpose? What next steps will be important for you to create momentum in realizing your Noble Purpose? How will you need to be different to live the truest expression of yourself? Record your responses in your journal or notepad. When finished, close your eyes. Be aware of the sounds outside and relax into the comfort this space affords you.

5. Noble Purpose Spiral Quality

Title one of your Noble Purpose cards, "Quality of (name a quality here) in the Noble Purpose Spiral." Take a look at your journal and identify those things to which you want to be especially more attentive in forwarding your Noble Purpose and service to others. Note the particular qualities of the Noble Purpose Spiral to which your beneficiary explicitly or implicitly refers. Consider what you might do to more effectively bring that quality of the spiral to bear on your life and work. Synthesize all of the thoughts that you want to continue to keep in your awareness on this card. Finally, relax and close your eyes. Breathe deeply. Follow your breath and allow it to carry you into the next moment and the completion of segment two of this process. Be aware of any tension you feel and release it.

Note: You may wish to leave this work, returning to Segment C of this process at another time. Plan now to return at a specific time, when you will be focused and prepared to begin the next segment of this process. Gather together the two Noble Purpose cards that you completed: "Noble Purpose Attributes" and "Quality of (name a quality here) in the Noble Purpose Spiral" and keep them with the cards from Segment A. You will return to these in Segment C of this process.

Segment C: Living Your Noble Purpose

As before, find a secluded, comfortable, quiet place away from others where you can visualize and journal. Again, you may wish to play soothing music to create an appropriate mood for reflection and writing.

1. Noble Purpose Statement

Close your eyes and fully relax. Take a deep breath. At this time, there is nothing to organize, nothing to grasp, nothing to do. Simply follow your breath and allow it to carry you into the next moment. Be aware of the chair you are seated on and how it supports you. Scan your body from the top of your head, slowly, to the bottom of your feet and release any tightness or stiffness you feel.

Based upon Segments A and B of this process, review your "Noble Purpose Statement" index card. Ask yourself the question, Does this Noble Purpose reflect your reason for being? Does it come authentically from your Essential Self (vs. your Bounded Self)? Say it out loud. Call friends and colleagues and assert your Noble Purpose to them. Ask for feedback. Do they get it? Is this statement of Noble Purpose the ultimate expression of your passion in life/work? If yes, go on to part two. If no, that's fine. It simply means you have more work to do to reveal your Noble Purpose. Notice which qualities of the Noble Purpose Spiral are missing for you. Seek support from a coach, colleagues or a family member to fully embrace that quality or qualities. If changes to your statement of Noble Purpose are needed, reflect on them now, creating a new card as necessary.

2. Noble Purpose Mindfulness List

Look over the Noble Purpose cards you prepared previously, including the "Noble Purpose Attributes" and "Quality of (name a quality here) in the Noble Purpose Spiral" cards. Next, brainstorm in your journal or notepad a "mindfulness" list for actions that you now see as important to bring forward your Noble Purpose. When complete, create a list of people who might be helpful in realizing what you are beginning to vision. Make the list as long as possible, checking your holiday card list, Rolodex, databases and address books of friends and colleagues. What specific requests do you want to make of the people identified on your list? Continue to add people and identify requests until you are complete. When finished, close your eyes. Take a deep breath. Follow your breath.

Imagine five years into the future, exploring and recording all of those places and ways that your Noble Purpose is living in the world. When complete, generate a list of either five timing and action steps or ways of being that would realize that long-term vision, in your journal or notepad. When finished, close your eyes and fully relax. Be aware of any tension you feel in your body and release it.

3. Noble Purpose Being and Action List

Title one of your Noble Purpose cards, "Noble Purpose Being and Action List." On this card list as many dimensions of being and/or action items, milestones and timing considerations as you possibly can. For example, on the being side, "To be compassionate in all aspects of my life/work," and on the action side, "To seek funding for my idea from the XYZ funding source." Take your time. Reflect on all parts of this process and all of your past experience regarding your Noble Purpose. Use as many cards as you feel appropriate, but focus on the immediate, here and now, on the first few cards. As before, relax, close your eyes and savor these qualities, realizing that they are an expression of your Essential Self. Take a minute or so to relax.

4. Noble Purpose Statement

You are nearing the end of your journey for all three segments of this process. There is just one final part. Place your "Noble Purpose Statement" card in front of you and reflect on how this statement embodies your Noble Purpose. Notice how your Noble Purpose intervenes in your life at the level of your Bounded Self. To the extent your Noble Purpose is a statement of who you are, identify a ritual (a symbolic act to invoke on a daily basis to celebrate and return yourself to your Noble Purpose). Note the ritual on your "Noble Purpose Being and Action List" card.

Now, once again consult your "Quality of (name a quality here) in the Noble Purpose Spiral" cards and your "Noble Purpose Attributes" cards and see if you wish to modify or change either your "Noble Purpose Statement" or "Timing and Action Steps." When complete, place a rubber band around your Noble Purpose cards, positioning your "Noble Purpose Statement" on top, followed by your "Noble Purpose Being and Action List." Place these cards in your purse, brief case, jacket pocket or in some other convenient place, consulting them on a daily basis. The key: stay fully conscious of your "Noble Purpose Statement" and your "Noble Purpose Being and Action List."

Noble Purpose as Generous Giving and Receiving: The Outer Level

An organization is a patchwork of human relationships, and you are a critical thread of that patchwork as is everyone around you. The patchwork also has its own Noble Purpose. The outer dimension of Noble Purpose brings you into contact with the larger patchwork of which you are an integral part — inseparable, interdependent, complete and whole. You are in service to the whole; the whole serves you.

If you operate from a place of scarcity, diminishing your gifts or the gifts of others, you impede the discovery and realization of your purpose. Personal and/or organizational prosperity and service to others will stagnate and, ultimately, wither without generous giving. Much ignoble behavior and decline of

Noble Purpose in the world can be traced to a fear that the more you give the less you will have.

Extraordinary Noble Purpose is essentially about generous service, contribution and giving. Giving out of a deep sense of love energizes you. You give freely, letting go of attachment to the outcome. There is an energetic exchange constantly taking place between giving and receiving that is the key to incredible prosperity. In giving comes great receiving.

Returning Home

Isn't life curious? You are bombarded with messages from the larger culture, advertisers, self-help books and often from your inner dialogue, that if ONLY you could change or be someone you are not, everything would be fine. Change. Change. Change. The simple truth — there is nothing to change; there is only the return to your deepest, Essential Self. Out of reuniting with your essence emerges the purest expression of your truth. As Mary Oliver, in her poem "Wild Geese," admonishes:

> *You do not have to be good.*
> *You do not have to walk on your knees*
> *for a hundred miles through the desert, repenting.*
> *You only have to let the soft animal of your body*
> *love what it loves.*

And Mary Oliver continues:

> *Meanwhile the wild geese, high in the clean blue air,*
> *are heading home again.*
> *Whoever you are, no matter how lonely,*
> *the world offers itself to your imagination,*
> *calls to you like the wild geese, harsh and exciting —*
> *over and over announcing your place*
> *in the family of things.*

As your path to extraordinary Noble Purpose is illuminated, you can become the path. The movement to becoming the path is not outward. It is inward to your essence and simultaneously everywhere, connecting with everything. Because you more fully drink in, partaking of your essence, you can at once be your purpose and brilliantly bring your purpose to the world.

Know that there is only to return home and that which is most authentic and unique in yourself will emerge. Have a great journey. Live life, love fully, nobly.

Exploring Noble Purpose In Your Daily Routine

> *Finding the courage to sing our own song*
> *Drawn from the wellspring within our own soul*
> *Piercing the darkness and shadows within*
> *Granting the spirit a home, again*

– Kathryn Hall

You may wish to revisit the processes from any of the preceding chapters for integrating Noble Purpose or some particular quality of the Noble Purpose Spiral into your daily routine. Here are some final Noble Purpose processes that you might want to incorporate into your daily routine. In addition to an affirmation, you will also find an anchoring activity, body exercise, ritual, journal writing or aesthetic appreciation, described as follows.

Affirmation

Create an affirmation that emphasizes and/or strengthens a particular implication of this chapter that would assist you in your journey to Noble Purpose. Write the affirmation on an index card or a piece of paper and carry it with you today. Repeat the affirmation several times before lunch, before ending your workday and before retiring in the evening.

For example, "I know that in giving is receiving and from this day forward I will give generously to those around me."

Anchoring Activity

Explore Noble Purpose in your life and approach the exploration in a non-analytical, organic way. Be playful. Keep it light. For example, take time to walk in your favorite place in nature today, for a half hour. As you begin your walk, consider what it means to provide Noble Purpose. What is Noble Purpose for you? Refrain from getting too logical. Allow thoughts and ideas to emerge. As you continue on your walk, release the question of Noble Purpose and allow yourself to just be, enjoying the place you are exploring. Along the way, notice objects in nature. Allow yourself to be drawn to one of these objects that is symbolic of Noble Purpose for you. Pick up an object (there may be more than one; choose the one that most "calls" to you) and return to your starting point. Record your thoughts on paper about the object from nature. Don't get too analytical, just let the object speak to you. Ask yourself: How is this object from nature symbolic of Noble Purpose for me? What does Noble Purpose mean to me? How does it exist in my life?

Body Exercise

Sit quietly for 10-15 minutes, releasing your thoughts and closing your eyes. Consider the following reflection, focusing on a particular body sensation.

Consider a time in your life when you were most successful in achieving extraordinary Noble Purpose. Return to that time. Be aware of your experience. Where did you experience your Noble Purpose in your body at that time? Did you feel it in your heart, head, back, stomach, legs, shoulders? Now, sit quietly and even more fully return yourself to that time of powerful Noble Purpose and to that place in your body. Notice: does that body sensation take on a shape, color, weight, mass and dimension? Experience it fully.

Ritual

Reflect on a time in your life when you were most contented with living your Noble Purpose. What were you doing? How were you being? Design a ritual that acknowledges that time and the circumstances of your life. For example, find an artifact that symbolizes that time in your life. You may want to locate a photo of yourself or the colleagues with whom you worked or create a collage from old magazines representing your great work. You can also find a product or an outward manifestation of your work at that time and place it prominently on your desk or in your workspace.

Journaling Activity

Reflect on your journey through life, returning to your childhood, moving thoughtfully and consciously through to the present. Notice the critical turning points along the way that were formative, leading you where you are today and guiding you in your pursuit of Noble Purpose. Avoid becoming too detailed. Look for major turning points. List these turning points and when complete, journal about the ebb and flow of your life and what created greatest momentum in your pursuit of Noble Purpose.

Rekindling Awareness for Noble Purpose Through Aesthetic Appreciation

There are many ways to rekindle your awareness for an important idea or thought that can change how you think or feel about some reality in your life or work. Three different forms of aesthetic expression are described below, one or more of which you may use to rekindle the ideas expressed in this chapter on Noble Purpose. The aesthetic forms include music, poetry and painting. These are only recommendations. You would be well served to reflect on various forms of aesthetic expression, choosing something you feel drawn to, and then using it to help embed the reality of Noble Purpose in your consciousness.

Music — Find a favorite piece of music that exemplifies Noble Purpose, and listen to it throughout the day, allowing the lyric or melody to enter your psyche, reinforcing the qualities associated with Initiating. Listen to the music on your drive to work, if feasible at work and/or at home at the end of the day.

I Can See Clearly Now is a song that is infused with the qualities associated with Noble Purpose:

"I can see clearly now the rain has gone; I can see all obstacles in my way; Gone are the dark clouds that had me blind; It's gonna be a bright, bright sunshiny day."

Poetry — Of your favorite poems, choose one that contains elements of Noble Purpose. Record the poem on an index card or a small piece of paper and place it in your pocket. Periodically throughout the day, find the poem and recite it to yourself and to significant others in your life.

"Poetics" is a poem by A. R. Ammons, that embodies the essential ideas of Noble Purpose. Here is a brief excerpt:

I look for the way
things will turn
out spiraling from a center ...

not so much looking for the shape
as being available
to any shape that may be
summoning itself
through me
from the self not mine but ours.

Painting — Consider your favorite paintings and choose a painting that evokes the quality of Noble Purpose for you. Notice how the use of color, texture, shape and form resonate within you and this quality of the Noble Purpose Spiral. Place the painting or a photo or other rendering of the painting in full view so that you can connect with it as you go through the day. If you cannot bring it to work with you, place it in a conspicuous place in your home, allowing it to provoke in you the qualities associated with Noble Purpose. If possible, capture the image of this painting electronically and save it as wallpaper on your personal computer so that it greets you throughout the day.

Appendix A

Claiming Process To Accomplish Noble Purpose

Achieving your Noble Purpose as revealed by Visioning requires you to break down the components of your mission into bite-sized action steps. The following process invites you to do just that. With each action step respond to a particular restraint that confronts you regarding your Noble Purpose or a project component of your Noble Purpose. The results should be stated in such a way that leaves no question as to whether or not it has been achieved. Results should be specific, measurable and attainable.

The format for designing your action steps requires you to methodically consider the restraining forces — those conditions and factors that tend to resist or constrain the realization of Noble Purpose, as well as the driving forces — those conditions and factors that tend to propel Noble Purpose forward. The notion of restraint comes from Kurt Lewin, who provides an infinitely practical organizational theory called "Force Field Analysis." Lewin identifies driving and restraining forces as critical implications of any change endeavor. See page 109 for a more detailed description of this useful theory. Begin by naming your Noble Purpose and identifying the critical project component that you wish to address. Using the process described in the following pages, brainstorm all of the restraints that you can think of that obscure your Noble Purpose. Claim action steps that serve to modulate or reduce the resistance in the form of the particular restraints you have identified. An "action step" is a pivotal step that diminishes a restraining force and leverages or promotes the accomplishment of the Noble Purpose project component. It may be useful to sketch out the components of the form in your journal or on notepaper in order to record your ideas. Allow one page for the first two column headings (i.e., restraints and action steps) and one page for the second two column headings (i.e., resources and timeline) so that you have sufficient space. Alternatively, attach a legal-size sheet of paper recording: restraints, action steps, resources and timeline.

ஜ *Claiming Form*

Noble Purpose: _____

Project Component: _____

Intended Outcome: _____

Restraints	Action Steps	Resources*	Timeline

*People and materials (regarding people, try to carefully formulate a network of support that will best fulfill your purpose)

Force Field Analysis

Lewin's Force Field Analysis holds that any change from one state to another state — which is often the case when fostering Noble Purpose — is characterized by movements of opposing forces, termed driving and restraining forces, as discussed earlier.

Common sense would suggest that increasing the intensity of the driving forces, so as to overcome the restraining forces, would be the best course of action. However, increasing the intensity of the driving forces frequently produces increased resistance from the restraining forces of approximately an equal magnitude.

Accordingly, Force Field Analysis suggests that you may be better served by systematically understanding and then modulating or altering the restraining force, thereby diminishing its resistance. This modulation of the restraining forces may take the form of individual or organizational resistance, requiring you to thoughtfully embrace and hear the position of others in such a way that the relationship is strengthened and there is an increased willingness to embrace different perspectives that express the value of your Noble Purpose. Movement toward the intended Noble Purpose can then be best accomplished by reducing the strength of the restraining forces while maintaining the driving forces.

✒ *Driving Forces vs. Restraining Forces*

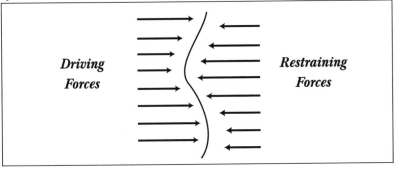

When Breakdowns Occur With Colleagues: A Letting Go Process

High-performing teams and organizations that embrace Noble Purpose out-produce the contributions of conventional teams. Extraordinary Noble Purpose results in more challenges and breakdowns. It requires a certain integrity to communicate authentically and to absolutely honor the perfection of views of others.

Such integrity requires you to be aware of how complete or incomplete you feel. Complete means that everything you need to say has been said. Incomplete means you have withheld communications that you are not sharing with others.

Such incompleteness is often a function of resignation that we feel toward others or situations. Resignation is defined as circumstances or persons who "are that way," typically an unfavorable way. No matter how inspired, Noble Purpose is greatly undermined when you are resigned about the situation, others or yourself. Such resignation may manifest itself as "playing it safe" or "holding on tightly."

Letting Go is expressing withheld feelings, which allows you to move to completeness and embrace your dissonance. Powerful Letting Go does not occur haphazardly. It must be carefully and respectfully conceived.

When dissonance occurs with a colleague, action is required to responsibly communicate the facts of the situation and the tension experienced. Letting go is also simultaneously listening to what others have to say, maintaining complete regard for the perfection of the other person. It requires us to listen fully and completely, even when a particular colleague may feel great frustration. Critically, such feedback is most effective when communicated from a place of high purpose, not from a complaint.

The following is a simple yet powerful process for organizing and communicating with others regarding dissonance and/or any breakdown you are experiencing.

1. State the high purpose of your communications.
2. Provide your observations of the relevant facts, issues, situation and/ or behaviors.
3. Describe your reactions.
4. Invite a response from your colleague.
5. State your understanding of what you are hearing.
6. Together, find ways to proceed and reach agreement about what to do.
7. Plan the next steps and offer your support.

The process appears simple. However, it requires a great deal of personal discipline. Old patterns of communicating are ingrained. Consciously work to avoid falling back into old patterns either unconsciously or out of frustration. When effectively used, this process can greatly help you deliver a difficult communication with a co-worker. Take the time to walk through each of the seven steps, particularly the first three, before you begin. Keep the emphasis on "I" statements, showing your ownership of the communication. Get yourself coached and with your coach do a trial run of what you want to say, getting feedback on your effectiveness. Also, don't assume that you can have this conversation any time, anywhere. Extend an invitation and with your colleague, choose an appropriate place and time.

Here are some tips for each of the seven steps in this process:

1. State the high purpose of your communications.

This is the critical starting place. If you aren't able to get to a place of high purpose regarding your communication and your colleague, don't deliver the communication. If your communication is parental or condescending of the other person, you can count that you won't make a difference. You may feel a great deal of angst about the situation, but coming from a negative place won't make anything happen. If necessary, get yourself coached on your purpose. Great purpose is grounded in authentic concern for your colleague, service, team, customer satisfaction, healing relationships, etc.

2. Provide your observations of the relevant facts, issues, situation and/or behaviors.

The focus here is on the facts — just the facts. Avoid melodrama. Focus on the realities at hand with the mantra when "x" then "y." Stay concise, without offering an evaluation. Focus on the situation, not the person.

3. Describe your reactions.

This is your opportunity to say how you feel about the facts, that is, the observations from step two. The idea is not to indulge your feelings. This part of the process by design comes after you have clarified your high purpose and observations. It should be short, to the point and fully authentic. For example: "I felt embarrassed, disappointed, angry, weary, upset."

4. Invite a response from your colleague.

It should not take long to get to this step of inviting a response, a minute at most as the first three points should be kept short and to the point. They should not be turned into a monologue. Your colleague may elect to respond sooner (there is no right time). The key here is to hear, fully and completely, what your colleague has to say. The response may be charged with emotion and full of melodrama. Your preparation is key — get in a space so that you can hear everything that needs to be said. This does not mean that you should necessarily cave in, or that you should purport to agree with something you don't. Develop the capacity to take it all in – examples of appropriate responses include: "I get it," "Yes, I hear that," "I understand," etc.

5. State your understanding of what you are hearing.

This is more of the same quality of listening described in step four. Be able to authentically respond: "What I hear you saying is _____ ," for all major points. Make sure your colleague knows that you have gotten his/her communications exactly as intended. This is key. Providing this space for your colleague can, in and of itself, completely transform your relationship.

6. Together, find ways to proceed and reach agreement about what to do.

Some conversations can lead to a breakthrough or a reconciliation as to what to do next. Other conversations, more typically, result in some compromise and accommodation. Whether the result is big or small, reach agreement concretely. Decide what you will do and what your colleague will do by when.

7. Plan the next steps and offer your support.

This is a key step in the process. Some people are so pleased to have gotten to some kind of accord that they abruptly end there. Step seven is key to building upon the work accomplished in steps one through six. Above all else, continue to develop the relationship. Be impeccable in following through on your agreements. Allow your colleague a lot of space as you renew your relationship and resolve the problem in follow-up meetings.

About the Author and the Noble Purpose Program

About the Author of Noble Purpose

Barry Heermann, Ph.D., is an organizational consultant and the creator of the Team Spirit team development program offered by the Plexus Corporation. Barry's Team Spirit program has been used in hundreds of organizations globally, including NCR, AT&T, General Motors, Volkswagen of America, LexisNexis and not-for-profits like Red Cross and United Way. He has served as a faculty member, department head, dean and vice president in public and private institutions, and he is the author of two books and three New Direction's editions published by Jossey-Bass on adult and experiential learning themes. His work with Team Spirit led to the McGraw-Hill book, *Building Team Spirit: Activities for Inspiring and Energizing Teams* (1997). Barry lives in Carmel-by-the-Sea, California, with his wife Kipra and dog Namaste.

About the Noble Purpose Program

This book, *Noble Purpose: Igniting Extraordinary Passion for Life and Work,* is one element of a comprehensive process for personal and professional development. The Noble Purpose program engages individuals in a probing exploration of their identity, values and purpose. A comprehensive curriculum includes a one-hour-a-day, week-long teleworkshop conducted by telephone; one-on-one coaching; a three-day, onsite experience; and a certification program for preparing Noble Purpose Learning Facilitators. The Noble Purpose program also includes a diagnostic component that provides feedback on individual Noble Purpose orientations, allowing individuals to plan actions tailored to their own needs.

For information about the Noble Purpose program offerings or to receive information about Noble Purpose go to www.NoblePurpose.com or call 1-888-753-9873.

Bibliography

Bohm, David. *Wholeness and the Implicate Order.* New York: Routledge, 1996.

Buckingham, Marcus and Curt Coffyian. *First Break All the Rules.* New York: Simon and Schuster, 1999.

Csikszentmihalyi, Mihaly. *Flow: The Psychology of Optimal Experience.* New York: Harper Collins Publishers, 1990.

Harvey, Andrew. *Sun at Midnight: A Memoir of the Dark Night.* New York: Tarcher/Putnam, 2002.

Hawkins, David R. *Power vs. Force — The Hidden Determinants of Human Behavior.* Sedona: Veritas Publishing, 1995.

Heermann, Barry. *Building Team Spirit.* New York: McGraw-Hill, 1997.

Henri, Robert. *The Art Spirit.* Boulder: Westview Press, 1984.

McDonald, Thomas P., editor. *A Thomas Merton Reader.* New York: Harcourt, Brace and World Inc., 1961.

Merton, Thomas. *New Seeds of Contemplation.* New York: New Directions, 1972.

Palmer, Parker J. *Let Your Life Speak: Listening for the Voice of Vocation.* San Francisco: Jossey-Bass, 2000.

Steindl-Rast, David. *Gratefulness, the Heart of Prayer — An Approach to Life in Fullness*. Mahwah: Paulist Press, 1984.

Steindl-Rast, David, and Sharon Lebell. *Music of Silence: A Sacred Journey Through the Hours of the Day*. Berkeley: Seastone, 1998.

Steindl-Rast, David. *Words of Common Sense For Mind, Body and Soul*. Randor: Templeton Foundation Press, 2002.

Vaill, Peter. *Managing as a Performing Art*. San Francisco: Jossey-Bass, 1989.

Note regarding underlying theory informing this book: The idea of essence, as well as boundedness, developed in Chapter Two, arises from Thomas Merton's "false self", "true self" distinction as described in *New Seeds of Contemplation* (1972) and editor T. P. McDonnell's *A Thomas Merton Reader* (1974) and from renowned physicist David Bohm's "implicate" and "explicate" orders of energy as described in *Wholeness and the Implicate Order* (1996). Bohm's notions of orders of energy were especially instructive in framing the potential of the Essential Self and also the Initiating, Visioning and Claiming qualities of the Noble Purpose Spiral.